Erich Fromm on Sigmund Freud:

Sex

"Freud, the great spokesman for sex, was altogether a typical puritan. To him, the aim of life for a civilized person was to suppress his emotional and sexual impulses."

Relation to women

"Paradoxical as it may appear, Freud was a man with a relatively weak interest in women, and with little sexual drive."

Psychoanalysis

"Freud's aim was to found a movement for the ethical liberation of man, a new secular and scientific religion for an elite which was to guide mankind."

SIGMUND FREUD'S MISSION

An Analysis of His Personality and Influence

By ERICH FROMM

GROVE PRESS, INC.   NEW YORK

Contents

I.

Freud's Passion for Truth
and His Courage

PSYCHOANALYSIS, as Freud liked to emphasize himself, was *his* creation. Its great achievements, as well as its defects, show the imprint of the founder's personality. No doubt, then, the origin of psychoanalysis is to be sought in Freud's personality.

What kind of man was he? What were the driving forces in him which made him act, think and feel in the particular way he did? Was he a decadent Viennese, rooted in the sensual and undisciplined atmosphere popularly held to be typically Viennese—as his enemies proposed—or was he the great master, in whom no personal shortcoming could be discovered, fearless and uncompromising in his search for truth, loving to his family, kind to his pupils and just to his enemies, without vanity or selfishness—as his most loyal adherents assert? Obviously, neither vilification nor hero worship is of much use to grasp the complex personality of Freud, nor to understand the impact of this personality on the structure of psychoanalysis. The same objectivity which Freud discovered as a necessary premise for the analysis of his patients is indispensable when we try to gain a picture of who he was and what motivated him.

The most striking and probably the strongest emotional force in Freud was *his passion for truth and his uncompromising faith in reason;* for him reason was the only human capacity which could help to solve the problem of existence or, at least, ameliorate the suffering which is inherent in human life.

Reason, so Freud felt, is the only tool—or weapon— we have to make sense of life, to dispense with illusions (of which, in Freud's thought, religious tenets are only one), to become independent of fettering authorities, and thus to establish our own authority. This faith in reason was the basis for his relentless pursuit of the truth, once he had seen a theoretical truth in the complexity and manifoldness of observable phenomena. Even if results, from the standpoint of common sense, seemed to be absurd, this did not disturb Freud. On the contrary, the laughing mob, whose thinking was determined by the wish for convenience and an undisturbed sleep, only accentuated the difference between conviction and opinion, reason and common sense, truth and rationalization.

In this faith in the power of reason, Freud was a child of the age of enlightenment. Its motto: *"Sapere aude"* —"Dare to know"—is stamped over all of Freud's personality and all of his work. It was a faith originally engendered in the emancipation of the Western middle class from the bonds and superstitions of feudal society. Spinoza and Kant, Rousseau and Voltaire, different as their philosophies were, all shared this passionate faith in reason; they all felt the common bond of fighting for a new, truly enlightened, free and human world. This spirit continued to exist in the nineteenth-century middle class of Western and Central Europe, and especially among the students devoted to the progress of the natural sciences. Freud's Jewish background,[1] if anything, added to his embrace of the enlightenment spirit. The Jewish tradition itself was one of reason and of intellectual discipline, and, besides that, a somewhat despised minority had a strong emotional interest to defeat the powers of darkness, of irrationality, of superstition, which blocked the road to its own emancipation and progress.

In addition to this general trend in the European intelligentsia of the late nineteenth century, there were specific circumstances in Freud's life which probably increased his tendency to rely on reason—and not on public opinion.

Quite in contrast to all great Western powers, the Austro-Hungarian monarchy was, in Freud's lifetime, a decaying body. It had no future, and the power of inertia, more than anything else, held the various parts of the monarchy together, in spite of the fact that her national minorities were frantically striving for independence. This

[1] The same point has been made by Helen Walker Puner in her excellent biography *Freud, His Life and His Mind*, Grosset and Dunlap, New York, 1943 (to be republished as a Dell-book in 1959). Her book is a most penetrating biography of Freud; in a number of important points, especially those of Freud's attitude to his Jewish background and of the quasi-religious character of the movement, my conclusions are very similar to the ones arrived at by her.

A profound analysis of Freud's relationship to his Jewish background is to be found in Ernst Simon's study, "Sigmund Freud, the Jew" (in *Yearbook II* of the publications of the Leo Baeck Institute, London, 1957, p. 270 ff.). I am also indebted to Professor Simon for reading the manuscript of this book, and for a number of critical suggestions.

state of political decay and dissolution was apt to awaken an intelligent boy's suspiciousness, and to arouse his questioning mind. The discrepancy between the official ideology and the *facts* of the political reality was apt to weaken anyone's confidence in the reality of words, slogans, authoritative statements, and was prone to foster the development of a critical mind. In Freud's special case, another element of insecurity must have furthered the same development. His father, a prosperous small manufacturer in Freiberg (Bohemia), had to give up his business as a result of the changes in the whole Austrian economy, which hit and impoverished Freiberg. Freud as a young boy learned by drastic experience that social stability was to be as little trusted as political stability; that no tradition or conventional setup offered any security or deserved confidence. For an extraordinarily gifted boy, where would these experiences lead him, but to put all his faith in himself, and in reason, as the only weapon he could dare to trust?

Yet there were many other boys growing up under the same circumstances, and they did not become Freuds; neither did they develop an extraordinary passion for truth. There must have been elements in Freud's personality, peculiar to himself, which were responsible for the extraordinary intensity of this quality.

What were they?

Undoubtedly we must first think of an intellectual endowment and a vitality, far above the average, which were part of Freud's constitution. This unusual intellectual gift, combined with the climate of the enlightenment philosophy, the shattering of the usual trust in words and ideologies—all this alone might be sufficient to explain

Freud's reliance on reason. There may be other purely personal factors, as, for instance, Freud's wish for prominence, which could have led to the reliance on reason, since no other power, be it money, social prestige or physical force, was at his disposal. If we look for still more personal elements in Freud's character which may account for his passion for truth, we must point to a negative element in his character, his lack of emotional warmth, closeness, love, and beyond that, of enjoyment of life. This may sound like a surprising statement to be made about the discoverer of the "pleasure principle," and the alleged protagonist of sexual pleasure, yet the facts speak with a loud enough voice so as not to leave any doubt. While I shall come back later to present some evidence for these statements, suffice it to say here that given his gifts, given the cultural climate, given the special European, Austrian and Jewish elements in his environment, a boy with his wish for fame and recognition and his lack of joy in life had to turn to the adventure in knowledge if he wanted to fulfill his life's desire. There may be still other personal elements which account for this side of Freud. He was a very insecure person, easily feeling threatened, persecuted, betrayed, and hence, as one would expect, with a great desire for certainty. To him, considering his whole personality, there was no certainty in love—there was only certainty in knowledge, and he had to conquer the world intellectually if he wanted to be relieved of doubt and the feeling of failure.

Jones, dealing with Freud's passion for truth as the "deepest and strongest motive in his nature, and the one which propelled him toward his pioneering achievements," attempts an explanation in line with orthodox psychoanalytic theory. According to that theory, Jones points out that the whole desire for knowledge "is fed by powerful motives arising in infantile curiosity about the primary facts of life" [2] (the meaning of birth and what has brought it about). I believe that in this assumption an unfortunate confusion is made: that between curiosity and the belief in reason. In persons with marked personal curiosity an early and particularly strong sexual curiosity may be found—but there seems to be little connection between this factor and a passionate thirst for truth. Another factor which Jones mentions is not much more convincing. Freud's half-brother Phillip was a man given to joking, "whom Freud suspected to be his mother's mate and whom he tearfully begged not to make his mother again pregnant. Could one trust such a man, who evidently knew all the secrets, to tell the truth about them? It would be a curious trick of fate, if this insignificant little man—he is said to have ended up as a peddler—had through his mere existence proved to have fortuitously struck the spark that lit the future Freud's determination to trust himself alone, to resist the impulse to believe others more than in himself, and in this way to make imperishable the name of Freud." [3] Indeed, it would be a "curious trick of fate"—if Jones were right. But is it not an extraordinary oversimplification, to "explain" Freud's spark with the existence of a somewhat distrusted half-brother and his sexual jokes?

In speaking of Freud's passion for truth and reason, one point must be mentioned here, although it will be

[2] Ernest Jones, *The Life and Work of Sigmund Freud,* Basic Books, Inc., New York, 1955, Vol. II, p. 433.
[3] *Ibid.,* p. 434.

developed further when we have arrived at a fuller picture of Freud's character: for him reason was confined
to *thought*. Feelings and emotions were per se irrational,
and hence inferior to thought. The enlightenment philosophers in general shared in this contempt for feeling and
affect. Thought was for them the only vehicle of progress
and reason to be found only in thought. They did not
see, as Spinoza had seen, that affects, like thought, can
be both rational and irrational and that the full development of man requires the rational evolution of *both*
thought and affect. They did not see that, if man's thinking is split from his feeling, both his thinking *and* his feeling become distorted, and that the picture of man based
on the assumption of this split is also distorted.

These rationalistic thinkers believed that if man understood intellectually the causes for his misery, this intellectual knowledge would give him the power to change
the circumstances which caused his suffering. Freud was
much influenced by this attitude, and it took him years
to overcome the expectation that the mere intellectual
knowledge of causes for neurotic symptoms would bring
about their cure.

Speaking of Freud's passion for truth would leave an
incomplete picture if one did not mention at the same
time one of his most extraordinary qualities, his *courage*.
Many people have, potentially, a passion for reason and
for truth. What makes it so difficult to realize this poten-
tial is that it requires courage—and this courage is rare.
The courage which is involved here is of a special kind.
It is not primarily the courage to risk one's life, freedom
or property, although this courage too is rare. The courage

to trust reason requires risking isolation or aloneness, and
this threat is to many even harder to bear than the threat
to life. Yet the pursuit of the truth by necessity exposes
the searcher to this very danger of isolation. Truth and
reason are opposed to common sense and public opinion.
The majority cling to convenient rationalizations and to
the views that can be glimpsed from the surface of things.
The function of reason is to penetrate this surface, and
to arrive at the essence hidden behind that surface; to
visualize objectively, that is, without being determined by
one's wishes and fears, what the forces are which move
matter and men. In this attempt one needs the courage
to stand the isolation from, if not the scorn and ridicule
of, those who are disturbed by the truth and hate the dis-
turber. Freud had this capacity to a remarkable degree.
He resented his isolation, he suffered from it, yet he was
never willing, or even inclined, to make the slightest
compromise which might have alleviated his isolation.
This courage was also his greatest pride; he did not think
of himself as a genius, but he appreciated his courage as
the most outstanding quality in his personality. This pride
may even sometimes have had a negative influence on his
theoretical formulations. He was suspicious of any theoretical formulation which might have sounded concili-
atory and, like Marx, he found a certain satisfaction in
saying things *pour épater le bourgeois* (to shock the
bourgeois). It is not easy to identify the sources of courage. To what extent is it a gift Freud was born with?
To what extent is it the result of a sense of his historical
mission, to what extent an inner strength related to his
position as the undisputed favorite son of his mother? In

all probability all three of these sources contributed to the development of Freud's extraordinary courage; but further appreciation of this as well as of other traits in Freud's personality must wait until we have arrived at a deeper picture of his character.

II.

His Relationship to His Mother;
Self-Confidence and Insecurity

THE understanding of the factors (aside from constitutional ones) which determine the development of any man's character must begin with his relatedness to his mother. Yet, in Freud's case, we know relatively little about this relationship. This fact, however, is in itself significant, because Freud himself was most sparing in his autobiographic endeavors in giving us information about his mother. Among the thirty-odd of his own dreams which he reports in *The Interpretation of Dreams* there are only two which deal with his mother. (A prolific dreamer, Freud must have had many more dreams about his mother, which he did not report.) They are both expressive of an intense attachment to her. The one, "dream of the three fates," goes as follows:

I went into a kitchen in search of some pudding. Three women were standing in it; one of them was the hostess of the inn and was twisting something about in her hand, as though she was making Knödel [dumplings]. She answered that I must wait till she was ready. (These were not definite spoken words.) I felt impatient and went off with a sense of injury. I put on an overcoat. But the first I tried on was too long for me. I took it off, rather surprised to find it was trimmed with fur. A second one that I put on had a long stripe with a Turkish design let into it. A stranger with a long face and a short pointed beard came up and tried to prevent my putting it on, saying it was his. I showed him then that it was embroidered all over with a Turkish pattern. He asked: "What have the Turkish (designs, stripes . . .) to do with you?" But we then became quite friendly with each other. [1]

In this dream we recognize the wish to be fed by Mother. (That the "hostess," or perhaps all three women, represent Mother becomes quite clear from Freud's associations to the dream.) The specific element in the dream is the impatience of the dreamer. When he was told that he must wait till she was ready, he "went off with a sense of injury." And what does he do then? He puts on a fur-trimmed coat which is too long for him—then another one which belongs to somebody else. We see in this dream the typical reaction of a mother-favored boy; he insists on being fed by Mother ("feeding" to be understood symbolically as "being cared for, loved, protected, admired," etc.). He is impatient and furious if he is not "fed" immediately, since he feels he has a right to immediate and complete attention. In his anger he walks out and usurps the role of the big man-father (symbol-

[1] Sigmund Freud, *The Interpretation of Dreams,* translated by James Strachey, Basic Books, Inc., New York, 1955, p. 204.

ized by the coat which is too long and belongs to a
stranger).

The other dream dealing with his mother is one of
Freud's infancy, from his seventh or eighth year, which
he still remembered and interpreted thirty years later. "I
saw my beloved mother, with a peculiarly peaceful, sleep-
ing expression on her features, being carried into the
room by two (or three) people with bird-beaks, and laid
upon the bed." [2] Freud remembers having awakened
from the dream in tears and screaming, an understandable anxiety if one considers that he was dreaming of his
mother's death. The fact that he remembered the dream
so vividly, after over thirty years, tends to show its significance; taking both dreams together, we see a boy, expecting from his mother that she fulfill all his wishes—
and deeply frightened at the idea that she could die.
However, the fact that these are the only two dreams
about his mother which Freud reports is in itself significant, looked at psychoanalytically; it tends to prove
Ernest Jones's suggestion "that in Freud's earliest years
there had been extremely strong motives for concealing
some important phase of his development—perhaps even
from himself. I would venture to surmise it was his deep
love for his mother." [3] The other facts we know about
Freud's life point in the same direction. That he was very
jealous of his brother Julius, who was born when he was
eleven months old, and that he never liked his two-and-
a-half-year-younger sister Anna may not be a sufficiently
specific datum to back up this hypothesis. But there are

[2] *Ibid.*, p. 583.
[3] Jones, *op. cit.*, Vol. II, p. 409.

other more specific and more striking facts. Most of all, his position of the favorite son, which is brought out very drastically by an event which happened when Freud's sister was about eight years old. Their mother, "who was very musical, got her to practice the piano, but, though it was at a certain distance from the 'cabinet,' the sound disturbed the young student Freud so much that he insisted on the piano being removed; and removed it was. So none of the family received any musical education, any more than Freud's children did later." [4] It is not hard to visualize the position the ten-year-old boy had acquired with his mother, when he could prevent the musical education of his family because he did not like the "noise" of music.[5]

The deep attachment to his mother is also expressed in Freud's later life. He, who aside from Tarok partners and colleagues hardly devoted any free time to anybody, including his wife, visited his mother every Sunday morning, and had her visit him every Sunday for dinner, until his old age.

This attachment to the mother and the role of being the admired, favored son has important implications for the development of character which Freud has seen himself, and reported in a probably autobiographical sense. "A man who has been the indisputable favorite of his mother keeps for life the feeling of a conquerer, that confidence

[4] *Ibid.*, Vol. I, p. 17.

[5] It is a characteristic example of the idolizing and unanalytic approach of Jones's biography that he comments that this incident is "an illustration of the esteem in which he and his studies were held in the family." This is, of course, a way of putting it—the conventional, common-sense way, rather than the analytic, dynamic one.

of success that often induces real success." [6] Mother's
love is by definition unconditional. She does not love her
child, as Father does, *because* he merits it, *because* of
what he has done, but because *he is* her child. Motherly
admiration for the son is unconditional too. She worships
and admires the son, not because of this or that which
he does, but because *he is* and because he is hers. This
attitude becomes more extreme if a son is the mother's
favorite and at the same time if the mother is more vital
and imaginative than the father, and thus rules in the
family, as seems to have been the case in Freud's family.[7]
Early motherly admiration gives that sense of victory and
success which Freud speaks of. It does not have to be
acquired, it cannot be doubted. This self-confidence takes
itself for granted, it expects respect and admiration, it
gives the impression of being superior to and not the equal
of the average man. Naturally one finds this type of
mother-conditioned, supreme self-confidence in exceed-
ingly gifted as well as in little-gifted persons. In the latter
case, we find, frequently, a tragicomic discrepancy between claims and gifts; in the former case a powerful
support for the development of a person's talents and
gifts. That Freud had this kind of self-confidence, and
that it was based on his attachment to his mother, is an
opinion also expressed by Jones. "This self-confidence,"
he writes, "which was one of Freud's prominent charac-
teristics, was only rarely impaired as he was doubtless
right in tracing it to the security of his mother's love." [8]

[6] S. Freud, *Collected Works,* Hogarth Press, London, 1952, Vol.
IV, p. 367.
[7] Cf. E. Simon, *op cit.,* p. 272.
[8] Jones, *op. cit.,* Vol. I, p. 5.

This intense attachment of Freud to his mother, most of which he concealed from others, and probably from himself, is of the greatest importance not only for the understanding of Freud's character, but also for the appreciation of one of his fundamental discoveries, that of the Oedipus complex. Freud explained the attachment to the mother—quite rationalistically—as being based on the sexual attraction of the little boy to the woman with whom he is most intimate. But, considering the intensity of his attachment to his own mother, and the fact that he tended to repress it, it is understandable that he interpreted one of the most powerful strivings in man, the craving for the care, protection, all-enveloping love and affirmation of Mother, as the more limited wish of the little boy to satisfy his instinctual needs through Mother. He discovered one of the most fundamental strivings in man, the wish to remain attached to Mother, and that is to the womb, to nature, to pre-individualistic, pre-conscious existence—and at the same time he negated this very discovery by restricting it to the small sector of instinctual desires. His own attachment to Mother was the basis of his discovery and his resistance to seeing his attachment was the basis for the limitation and distortion of this very discovery.[9]

But the attachment to Mother, even the very satisfactory one which implies indisputable confidence in Moth-

---

[9] It is interesting to note that Freud's great predecessor in the discovery of the power of the attachment to the mother, J. J. Bachofen, was also deeply attached to his mother. (He married when he was around forty, after his mother's death.) He did not, however, try to minimize the power of this emotional attachment but, on the contrary, revealed its significance in his theory of the matriarchate.

er's love, has not only the positive side of giving absolute
self-confidence, it has also the negative side of creating a
feeling of dependency, and of depression whenever the
euphorizing experience of unconditional love and admiration is not forthcoming. It seems that this dependency
and insecurity are central elements in the structure of
Freud's character, and of his neurosis.

Freud's insecurity found the expression so characteristic of the oral-receptive person, the fear of hunger, of
starvation. Because the receptive person's security rests
on the conviction of being fed, nursed, loved, admired
by Mother, his fears are concerned exactly with the possibility of this love failing.

In a letter to Fliess (December 21, 1899) Freud writes:
"My phobia, if you please, was a poverty or rather, a
hunger phobia, arising out of my infantile gluttony and
called up by the circumstances that my wife had no dowry
(of which I am proud)." [10] The same topic is touched
in another letter to Fliess (May 7, 1900). There Freud
says: "On the whole—except for one weak point,
my fear of poverty, I have too much sense to com-
plain. . . ." [11]

This fear of impoverishment found a strong expression
at one of the most dramatic points of Freud's career,
when he persuaded his Viennese, and mostly Jewish, colleagues to accept the leadership of the Zürich (and mostly
Gentile) analysts. When the Viennese did not want to
accept this proposal, Freud declared (1910): "My enemies would be willing to see me starve; they would tear

[10] Cf. *The Origins of Psychoanalysis,* letters to Wilhelm Fliess,
by Sigmund Freud, Basic Books, Inc., New York, 1954, p. 305.
[11] *Ibid.,* p. 318. (My italics. E. F.)

my very coat off my back." [12] This statement, even considering that it was meant to influence the hesitant Viennese, certainly was quite unrealistic, and is a symptom of the same fear of starvation Freud mentions in his letters to Fliess.

Freud's insecurity also found other expressions. The most obvious one is his fear connected with traveling on the railroad. He had to go to the station one hour before the train's departure, in order to be sure not to miss it. As always, if one analyzes such a symptom, one must understand its symbolic meaning. Traveling is often a symbol of leaving the security of mother and home, of being independent, cutting one's roots. Therefore, for people with a strong mother attachment, traveling is frequently experienced as dangerous, an enterprise for which one has to take very special precautions. For the same reason Freud also avoided traveling by himself. On his big trips during the summer vacations, he was always accompanied by a person on whom he could depend, usually one of his pupils, sometimes his wife's sister. It is also part of the same pattern of being afraid of cutting one's roots that Freud lived in the same apartment in the Berggasse from the time early in his marriage to the day of his forced emigration from Austria. We shall see later how this very dependence on his mother manifested itself in the relationship to his wife and also to men, older ones, contemporaries and disciples, upon whom he transferred the same need for unconditional love, affirmation, admiration, and protection.

---

[12] Quoted from Jones, *op. cit.*, Vol. II, pp. 69–70.

III.

Freud's Relationship to Women; Love

IT IS not surprising to find that Freud's dependency on a mother figure manifests itself also in his relationship to his wife. The most striking feature in this relationship is the contrast between his attitude before and after his marriage. During the years of his engagement, Freud was an ardent, passionate and extremely jealous lover. The following quotation from a letter to Martha (June 2, 1884) is a characteristic expression of the ardor of his love. "Woe to you, my Princess, when I come. I will kiss you quite red and feed you till you are plump. And if you are forward you shall see who is the stronger, a gentle little girl who doesn't eat enough or a big wild man who has cocaine in his body." [1]

The joking reference to "who is the stronger" has a very serious implication. In those years of engagement, Freud was possessed by the passionate wish to have complete control over Martha, and naturally, this wish also implied an intense jealousy of anybody in whom she could

[1] Quoted from Jones, *op. cit.*, Vol. I, p. 84.

have interest and affection besides himself. A cousin, Max Mayer, for instance, had been her first predilection. "There came a time when Martha was forbidden to refer to him as Max, only as Herr Mayer." [2] Or with regard to another young man, who had been in love with Martha, Freud wrote: "When the memory of your letter to Fritz and our day on the Kahlenberg comes back to me I lose all control of myself, and had I the power to destroy the whole world, ourselves included, to let it start all over again—even at the risk that it might not create Martha and myself—I would do so without hesitation." [3]

But Freud's jealousy was by no means restricted to other young men; it equally applied to Martha's affectionate feelings for her family. He demanded from her "that she should not simply be able to criticize her mother and brother objectively and abandon their 'foolish superstitions,' all of which she did, but she had also to withdraw all affection from them—this on the grounds that they were his enemies, so that she should share his hatred of them." [4]

The same spirit is to be found in Freud's reaction to Martha's brother Eli. Martha had entrusted him with a sum of money, which she had, and which she and her fiancée wanted to use to buy the furniture for their apartment. It seems Eli had invested the money and was hesitant to return the whole amount immediately, but proposed that they buy the furniture on installments. In reaction to this, Freud addressed an ultimatum to Martha,

[2] *Ibid.*, p. 110.
[3] *Ibid.*, pp. 114–15.
[4] *Ibid.*, p. 123.

the first point of which was that she had to write an angry letter to her brother, and to call him "a scoundrel." Even after Eli had paid the money, Freud demanded that she "was not to write him [Freud] again, until she promised to break off all relations with Eli." [5]

This assumption of the natural right of the man to control his wife's life was part of Freud's views on male superiority. A typical example of this attitude is his criticism of John Stuart Mill. Freud praises Mill for being "perhaps the man of the century who best managed to free himself from the domination of customary prejudices. On the other hand . . . he lacked in many matters the sense of the absurd." [6] And what was so "absurd in Mill's ideas? According to Freud, it was his view "of female emancipation and . . . the woman's question altogether." The fact that Mill thinks that a married woman could earn as much as her husband makes Freud say:

> That is altogether a point with Mill where one simply can not find him human. . . . It is really a stillborn thought to send women into the struggle for existence exactly as men. If, for instance, I imagined my gentle sweet girl as a competitor, it would only end in my telling her, as I did seventeen months ago, that I am fond of her and that I implore her to withdraw from the strife into the calm uncompetitive activity of my home. . . . I believe that all reforming in law and education would break down in front of the fact that, long before the age at which a man can earn a position in society, nature has

[5] *Ibid.*, p. 137.
[6] *Ibid.*, p. 176.

determined woman's destiny through beauty, charm and sweetness. Law and custom have much to give women that has been withheld from them, but the position of women will surely be what is is: in youth an adored darling, and in mature years a loved wife.[7]

Freud's views on the subject of the emancipation of women are certainly not different from the views held by the average man in Europe in the eighties. But Freud was not an average man, he rebelled against some of the most deeply ingrained prejudices of his time, yet in this aspect he repeats the most conventional line on the problem of women, and calls Mill "absurd" and "inhuman" for views which not more than fifty years later were accepted quite generally. This attitude certainly shows how strong and compelling Freud's need was to put women in an inferior place. That his theoretical views mirrored this attitude is obvious. To look at women as castrated men, with no genuine sexuality of their own, always jealous of men, with a weakly developed Super-Ego, vain and unreliable, all this is an only slightly rationalized version of the patriarchal prejudices of his times. A man like Freud, with the ability to look through and criticize conventional prejudices, must have been determined by strong forces within himself, not to see the rationalizing character of these allegedly scientific statements.[8]

Freud still held the same opinions fifty years later. When he criticized American culture for its "matriarchal" character, his visitor and student, Dr. Worthis, answered:

[7] Letter to Martha (November 5, 1883), quoted by Jones, *op cit.*, Vol. I, p. 177.

[8] Cf. Jones, *op. cit.*, Vol. II, p. 421.

"But don't you think that it would be the best if both partners were equal?" To which Freud replied: "That is a practical impossibility. *There must be inequality* and the superiority of the man is the lesser of two evils." [9]

While the years of Freud's engagement were full of fiery wooing and jealous cajoling, his married life seems to have lacked active love and passion to a considerable degree. As in so many conventional marriages, the conquest is exciting, but once the conquest is made, there is no strong source of a passionate feeling of love. Male pride is involved in courtship; after marriage pride does not find any further satisfaction. There is only one function which the wife has to fulfill in this type of marriage: that of the mother. She must be unconditionally devoted to the husband, care for his material welfare, always be subordinate to his needs and wishes, always be the woman who wants nothing for herself, the woman who waits—that is, Mother. Freud was ardently in love before his marriage—because he had to prove his manliness by the conquest of the girl he had chosen. Once the conquest was sealed by the marriage, the "adored darling" was transformed into the loving mother on whose care and love one could depend without an active, passionate love for her.

How receptive and lacking in erotic passion Freud's love for his wife was, is amply demonstrated by a number of significant details. Most impressive of all these details are his letters to Fliess. There is hardly any mention of his wife, except in a purely conventional context. Con-

---

[9] J. Worthis, *Fragment of an Analysis with Freud,* Simon & Schuster, New York, 1954, p. 98. (Italics mine. E. F.)

sidering the fact that Freud writes in the greatest detail about his ideas, his patients, his professional successes and disappointments, this is in itself quite significant; but more important than this is the fact that Freud often describes in a depressed mood the emptiness of his life, which is filled out and satisfactory for him only when his work goes on successfully. Never does he mention his relationship to his wife as an important source of happiness. The same picture is obtained when one considers Freud's way of spending his time at home or on vacation. On week-days Freud saw patients from eight to one, then he had lunch, took a walk alone, worked in his consultation room from three to nine or ten, then took a walk with his wife, sister-in-law or daughter, then worked on his correspondence and writing until one A.M., unless there was a meeting that evening. The meals seem to have been not particularly sociable. A good example is Freud's habit "of bringing his latest purchase of an antiquity, usually a small statuette, to the dinner table, and placing it in front of him as a companion during the meal. Afterward, it would be returned to his desk, and then brought back again for a day or two." [10] On Sundays, Freud visited his mother in the morning, was with analytic friends and colleagues in the afternoon, had his mother and sisters for dinner, and then worked on his manuscripts.[11] His wife used to have visits from friends in the afternoon, and it is a rather telling comment on Freud's active interest in his wife's life that Jones reports that if his wife's visitors included "anyone in whom Freud

[10] Jones, *op. cit.*, Vol. II, p. 393.
[11] *Ibid.*, p. 384.

was interested he would drop into the drawing room for a few minutes." [12]

Freud spent a great deal of time in the summer traveling. This vacation period was the great occasion to compensate for the period of hard and continuous work during the rest of the year. Freud loved to travel, and he disliked traveling alone. But the vacation time was used to make up only partly for the little time he spent with his wife at home. As mentioned before, he traveled abroad with his psychoanalytic friends, or even with his wife's sister, but not with his wife. There are several explanations given for this fact, one by himself and one by Jones. The latter writes that "his wife, busy with other duties, was seldom mobile enough to travel, nor was she equal to Freud's restless pace or his omnivorous passion for sightseeing. . . . But almost every day on such tours he would send a postcard or telegram to her and every few days a long letter." [13] Again, it is remarkable how conventional and unanalytical Jones's thinking becomes when its object is his hero. Any man who enjoys spending his free time with his wife would just curb his passion for sightseeing enough to make it possible for his wife to participate. The rationalizing quality of these explanations is made even clearer, because of the fact that Freud gives a different reason why he did not travel with his wife. In a letter from Palermo, where he was with Ferenczi, he wrote to his wife:

I am desperately sorry not to let all of you see the beautiful things here. To be able to enjoy such things

---

[12] *Ibid.*, (My italics. E. F.)
[13] *Ibid.*, Vol. II, p. 15.

in the company of seven or nine, or even of three, I
should have been not a psychiatrist and allegedly the
founder of a new direction in psychology, but a
manufacturer of something useful like toilet paper,
matches or boot-buttons. It is too late to learn that
now, so I have to go on enjoying myself egotistically,
but with a deep sense of regret.[14]

Needless to say that Freud engages here in typical rationalizations, practically the same as those used by other
husbands who enjoy their vacations more in the company
of male friends than in that of their wives. The remarkable thing, again, is how blind Freud was, in spite of his
auto-analyzing, to the very problem of his marriage, and
how he rationalizes without the slightest awareness of
what he is doing. He speaks of nine or seven or even three
he would have to take with him, when it is all a matter of
taking his wife, which makes two; he then has to pose as
the poor but important scientist rather than the rich
manufacturer of toilet paper—all in order to explain why
he did not want to take his wife abroad.

Perhaps the clearest expression of the problematic
nature of Freud's love is contained in a dream, published
in *The Interpretation of Dreams*.[15] This is the dream: "*I
had written a monograph on a certain plant. The book
lay before me and I was at the moment turning over a
folded colored plate. Bound up in each copy there was a
dried specimen of the plant, as though it had been taken
from a herbarium.*" From Freud's associations I mention

[14] Letter of September 15, 1910, quoted by E. Jones, *op. cit.*,
Vol. II, p. 394.
[15] P. 169 ff.

the following: "That morning I had seen a new book in the window of a bookshop, bearing the title *The Genus Cyclamen*—evidently a monograph on that plant. Cyclamen, I reflected, were my wife's *favorite flowers* and I reproached myself for so rarely remembering to *bring* her *flowers* which was what she liked."

Another chain of dream associations leads Freud from the flower to a quite different topic, that of his ambition. "Once I recalled I really *had* written something in the nature of a *monograph on a plant,* namely a dissertation on the *coca plant* which had drawn Karl Koller's attention to the anaesthetic properties of cocaine." Freud then thinks of a *Festschrift* in honor of Koller, one editor of which he had met the night before. This association about cocaine is related to Freud's ambition. He expresses in other connections how sorry he was to have left the pursuit of the coca problem, and thus to have lost the chance for making a great discovery. This is also brought up in connection with the fact that he had to give up pure research in order to get married.

The meaning of the dream is quite clear (although Freud does not see it in his own interpretation). The *dried specimen* of the plant is the central point, and it expresses the conflict within Freud. A flower is a symbol of love and joy, especially since this flower is the favorite flower of his wife, which he seldom remembers to bring her. But the coca plant stands for his scientific interest and his ambition. What does he do with flowers, with love? He presses them, and puts them into a herbarium. That is, he lets love dry, and makes it the object of a scientific examination. This is exactly what Freud did. He made love an object of science, but in his life it remained dry and sterile. His scientific-intellectual interests were stronger than his eros; they smothered it, and at the same time became a substitute for his *experience* of love.

The impoverishment of love as expressed in this dream refers also quite clearly to his erotic and sexual desires and capacities. Paradoxical as it may appear, Freud was a man with a relatively weak interest in women, and with little sexual drive. It is perfectly true that, as Jones states, "his wife was assuredly the only woman in Freud's love life," and that "she always came first before all other mortals." [16] But Jones also points out that "it is likely that the more passionate side of life subsided with him earlier than it does with many men." [17] The truth of this statement is backed up by several facts. Freud, at forty-one, wrote to Fliess, complaining about his moods and then adding: "Also sexual excitation is of no more use to a person like me." [18] Clearly, at this age sexual life had more or less ended for him. Another incident points to the same fact. Freud reports in *The Interpretation of Dreams* that one time, in his forties, he felt physically attracted to a young woman and half-voluntarily touched her slightly. He comments that he was surprised to "still" find the possibility for such attraction in him. At the age of fifty-six he wrote to L. Binswanger: "Today, naturally, the libido of the old man exhausted itself by distributing money." Even at this age, only a man whose sexual life was of little intensity would take it for granted that his libido had given up sexual aims.

[16] Jones, *op. cit.*, Vol. II, p. 386.
[17] *Ibid.*
[18] *The Origins of Psychoanalysis,* ed. by M. Bonaparte, A. Freud, E. Kris, Basic Books, Inc., New York, 1954, p. 227; letter to Fliess, 31. 10. 97.

If some speculation is in order, I would be prone to assume that some of Freud's theories are also proof for his inhibited sexuality. He has emphasized repeatedly that sexual intercourse can give only limited satisfaction to civilized man, "that the sexual life of civilized man is seriously disabled," that "one is probably right in supposing that the importance of sexuality as a source of pleasurable sensations, i.e., as a means of fulfilling the purpose of life, has perceptibly decreased." [19] He accounts for this fact by the hypothesis that full satisfaction is possible only if the pregenital, olfactory and other "perverse" strivings are not repressed, and went even so far as to think of the possibility that "it is not only the oppression of culture, but something in the nature of the [sexual] function itself, that denies us full satisfaction and urges us in other directions." [20]

Furthermore, Freud believed that after "three, four or five years marriage ceases to furnish the satisfaction of the sexual needs that it promised, since all the contraceptives available hitherto impair sexual enjoyment, disturb the finer susceptibilities of both partners, or even act as a direct cause of illness." [21]

Considering Freud's remarks about his sexual life, it can be surmised that these views about sex were the rationalizing expression of his own inhibited sexuality. Undoubtedly there were many men of his social class, age and general culture who did not feel in their forties that

[19] S. Freud, *Civilization and Its Discontents*, translated by J. Riviere, The Hogarth Press, Ltd., London, 1953, p. 76.
[20] *Ibid.*, pp. 76–77.
[21] "Civilized Sexual Morality and Modern Nervousness," *Collected Papers*, II, 89.

the period of happiness derived from sexual relations was over, and who would not have shared with him the view that after a few years of marriage sexual happiness ceased to exist, even considering the necessity of using contraceptives.

Going a step further, we may also surmise that another theory of Freud had a rationalizing function: his thesis that civilization and culture were the result of the suppression of the instincts. What he was saying in this theory was, in so many words: because I am so concerned with thought and truth, I necessarily have little interest in sex. Freud, here as so often, generalized an individual experience. *He* happened to suffer from a sexual inhibition for other reasons, but not *because* he was so deeply concerned with creative thought. Freud's sexual inhibitedness may sound like a contradiction to the fact that in his theories Freud gave such a central place to the sexual drive. But this contradiction is more apparent than real. Many thinkers write about what they lack, and what they strive to achieve for themselves—or for others. Furthermore, Freud, a man of puritan attitude, would hardly have been able to write so frankly about sex had he not been so sure of his own "goodness" in this respect.

Freud's lack of emotional closeness to women is also expressed in the fact that he understood little of women. His theories about them were naïve rationalizations of male prejudices, especially of the male who needs to dominate in order to hide his fear of women. But Freud's lack of understanding of women need not be concluded from his theories only. He once stated it himself with remarkable frankness, when he said in a conversation: "The great question that has never been answered, and which

I have not been able to answer, despite my thirty years of research into the feminine soul, is what does a woman want? [*Was will das Weib?*]" [22]

But in speaking about Freud's capacity to love we must not confine ourselves to the problem of erotic love. Freud had little love for people in general, when no erotic component was involved. His relationship to his wife, after the ardor of the first conquest had burned out, was apparently that of a faithful but somewhat distant husband. His relationship to his male friends, Breuer, Fliess, Jung and his faithful students, was also distant. In spite of the idolizing descriptions by Jones and Sachs, one must be convinced by his letters to Fliess, his reactions to Jung and eventually to Ferenczi, that it was not given to Freud to have a strong experience of love. His own theoretic views only confirm this. Concerning the possibility of brotherly love, he says,

> We may find the clue in one of the so-called ideal standards of civilized society. It runs: "Thou shalt love thy neighbour as thyself." It is world-renowned, undoubtedly older than Christianity which parades it as its proudest profession, yet certainly not very old; in historical times men still knew nothing of it. We will adopt a naïve attitude towards it, as if we were meeting it for the first time. Thereupon we find ourselves unable to suppress a feeling of astonishment, as at something unnatural. Why should we do this? What good is it to us? Above all, how can we do such a thing? How could it possibly be done? My love seems to me a valuable thing that I have no

right to throw away without reflection. It imposes obligations on me which I must be prepared to make sacrifices to fulfill. If I love someone, he must be worthy of it in some way or other. (I am leaving out of account now the use he may be to me, as well as his possible significance to me as a sexual object; neither of these two kinds of relationship between us come into question where the injunction to love my neighbour is concerned.) He will be worthy of it if he is so like me in important respects that I can love myself in him; worthy of it if he is so much more perfect than I that I can love my ideal of myself in him; I must love him if he is the son of my friend, since the pain my friend would feel if anything untoward happened to him would be my pain—I should have to share it. But if he is a stranger to me and cannot attract me by any value he has in himself or any significance he may have already acquired in my emotional life, it will be hard for me to love him. I shall even be doing wrong if I do, for my love is valued as a privilege by all those belonging to me; it is an injustice to them if I put a stranger on a level with them. But if I am to love him (with that kind of universal love) simply because he, too, is a denizen of the earth, like an insect or an earthworm or a grass-snake, then I fear that but a small modicum of love will fall to his lot and it would be impossible for me to give him as much as by all the laws of reason I am entitled to retain for myself. What is the point of an injunction promulgated with such solemnity, if reason does not recommend it to us? [23]

[23] Sigmund Freud, *Civilization and Its Discontents,* pp. 81–82.

Freud, the great spokesman for sex, was altogether a typical puritan. To him, the aim of life for a civilized person was to suppress his emotional and sexual impulses, and at the expense of this suppression, to lead a civilized life. It is the uncivilized mob which is not capable of such sacrifice. The intellectual elite are those who in contrast to the mob were capable of not satisfying their impulses, and thus sublimating them for higher purposes. Civilization as a whole is the result of such non-satisfaction of instinctual impulses.

It is remarkable how the ideas expressed in Freud's later theories were already alive in him as a young man, when he was not yet concerned with problems of history and sublimation. In a letter to his fiancée he describes a train of thought that had occurred to him during the performance of *Carmen.* "The mob," he writes,

give vent to their impulses [*sich ausleben*], and we deprive ourselves. We do so in order to maintain our integrity. We economize with our health, our capacity for enjoyment, our forces: we save up for something, not knowing ourselves for what. And this habit of constant suppression of natural instincts gives us the character of refinement. We also feel more deeply and therefore dare not demand much of ourselves. Why do we not get drunk? Because the discomfort and shame of the hangover [*Katzenjammer*] gives us more "unpleasure" than the pleasure of getting drunk gives us. Why don't we make a friend of everyone? Because the loss of him or any misfortune happening to him would bitterly affect us. *Thus our striving is more concerned with avoiding pain than with creating enjoyment.* When the effort succeeds, those who deprive themselves are like us, who have bound ourselves for life and death, who endure privation and yearn for each other so as to keep our troth, and who would assuredly not survive a hard blow of fate that would rob us of our dearest: human beings who like Asra can love only once. Our whole conduct of life presupposes that we shall be sheltered from the direst poverty, that it is always open to us to free ourselves increasingly from the evils of our social structure. The poor, the common people, could not exist without their thick skin and their easygoing ways. Why should they feel their desires intensely when all the afflictions nature and society have in store are directed against those they love: why should they scorn a momentary pleasure when no other awaits them? The poor are too powerless, too exposed, to do as we do. When I see the people doing themselves well, putting all seriousness aside, it makes me think it is their compensation for being so unprotected against all the imposts, epidemics, diseases, and the evil conditions of our social organization. I will not follow these thoughts further, but one might show how *das Volk* judges, believes, hopes, and works quite otherwise than we do. There is a psychology of the common man which is somewhat different from ours. Such people also have more feeling of community than we do: it is only they who are alive to the way in which one life is the continuation of the next, whereas for each of us the world vanishes with his death.[24]

This letter of the young Freud, at the age of twenty-seven years, is interesting in various aspects. Anticipating his later theories Freud expresses in this letter his puritan-aristocratic orientation which we have just discussed: to deprive oneself, to economize with one's capacity for enjoyment is the condition of sublimation, the basis on which an elite is formed. But beyond that, Freud exhibits here a view which was to become the basis of one of his most important theories to be developed many years later. He describes his fear of being hurt emotionally. We don't love everybody, because the parting would be so painful; we don't make friends of everyone, because the loss of a friend would cause us sadness. Life is oriented in the direction of avoiding sadness and pain, rather than of experiencing joy. As Freud says it clearly himself: "Thus our striving is more concerned with avoiding pain than with creating enjoyment." We find here the formulation of what Freud later called the "pleasure principle"; this idea, that pleasure is really relief from unpleasure, from painful tension, rather than positive enjoyment, appeared in later years to Freud as a generally valid, in fact, as the most general and basic, principle of human motivation. Yet, we can see here that Freud had this same idea years before this theoretical concern, and he had it as a result of his own Victorian personality, afraid of loss of possession (in this case of a love object and the *feeling* of love)—and in a way, of life. This atti-

[24] Letter to his fiancée of August 29, 1883, quoted by Jones, *op. cit.*, Vol. I, pp. 190–92. (Italics mine. E. F.)

tude was characteristic of the nineteenth-century middle
class, which was more concerned with "to have" than
with "to be." Freud's psychology was deeply imbued with
this orientation of "to have," and hence the deepest fears
for him are always the fear of losing something one "has,"
be it a love object, a feeling or the genital organ. (In this
respect he did not share the protest against middle-class
possessiveness which we find for instance in Goethe's
philosophy.)

One other paragraph in this letter needs to be emphasized. Freud says of the common people that they
have more feeling of community than "we do." "It is only
they who are alive to the way in which one life is the continuation of the next, whereas for each of us the world
vanishes with his death." Freud's observation that the
bourgeoisie has less of a feeling of solidarity than the
working class is quite true, but one must not forget that
there were many individuals in the middle and upper
classes who had a deep sense of human solidarity, either
socialists, anarchists or truly religious people. Freud had
little or none of it. He was concerned with *his* person, *his*
family, *his* ideas, in the fashion characteristic of the middle class. It is in the same vein that, seventeen years later,
on the occasion of the New Year, 1900, he writes to his
friend Fliess: "The new century—*the most interesting
thing about which for us is, I dare say, that it contains
the date of our death*—has brought me nothing but a
stupid review." [25] Here again we find the same egocentric
concern with his own death and none of the feeling of
universality and solidarity which he ascribes only to the
lower classes.

[25] *The Origin of Psychoanalysis,* p. 307. (My italics. E. F.)

IV.

His Dependence on Men

FREUD'S dependency on the mother figure was not restricted to his wife and his mother. It was transferred to men, older ones like Breuer, contemporaries like Fliess and pupils like Jung. But Freud had a fierce pride in his independence and a violent aversion to being the protégé. This pride made him repress the awareness of dependency and negate it completely by breaking off the friendship when the friend failed in the complete fulfillment of the motherly role. Thus his great friendships follow the same rhythm: intense friendship for several years, then complete break, usually to the point of hatred. This was the fate of his friendship with Breuer, Fliess, Jung, Adler, Rank and even Ferenczi, the loyal pupil who never dreamed of separating himself from Freud and his movement.

Breuer, an older and successful colleague, had given Freud the seed of the idea which was to develop into psychoanalysis. Breuer had been treating a patient, Anna O., and discovered that whenever he put her into hypnosis and made her tell him what was bothering her, she would feel relieved of her symptoms (depression and confusion). Breuer understood that the symptoms were caused by an emotional upheaval she had experienced while nursing her sick father, and furthermore, he understood that the irrational symptoms were meaningful once one understood their origin. Thus Breuer gave Freud the most important suggestion he ever received in his life, a suggestion which formed the basis of the central idea of psychoanalysis. Beyond that, Breuer acted toward Freud as a fatherly friend, including also not inconsiderable material help. How did this relationship end? True, there was a developing theoretical disagreement, because Breuer did not follow Freud in all this theories about sex. But certainly such theoretical disagreement would not normally lead to a personal break, not to speak of the hatred Freud felt toward his former friend and benefactor. Or to put it in Jones's words: "The scientific differences alone can not account for the bitterness with which Freud wrote about Breuer in the Fliess correspondence in the nineties. When one recollects what Breuer had meant to him in the eighties, his generosity to Freud, his understanding sympathy and the combination of cheerfulness and intellectual stimulation that radiated from him, the change later is indeed startling." [1]

The remarks which Freud makes about Breuer are quoted by Jones from unpublished letters to Fliess.[2] Freud writes on February 6, 1896, that "it was impossible to get on any longer with Breuer." A year later (March 29, 1897) he wrote that "the very sight [of Breuer] would

[1] Jones, op. cit., Vol. I, pp. 254-55.
[2] The letter mentioned here is not published in the volume of Freud's letters to Fliess (The Origins of Psychoanalysis).

make me inclined to emigrate." Jones comments: "These are strong words and there are stronger ones which need not be reproduced." [3] How little Breuer reacted in the same spirit can be seen from the fact that when Freud wanted to pay his debt, Breuer suggested that it be set off against an amount he considered Freud should be paid for medical attention to a relative of his.

How can we explain this change from love to loathing in Freud's relationship to Breuer? According to Freud himself, and Jones follows him in this characteristically orthodox interpretation, this ambivalence was the continuation, and repetition, of Freud's ambivalence toward his nephew, who was a little older than himself, when they were both children. But here, as so often when Freudian interpretation seeks to understand later developments as mere repetitions of infantile patterns, the true meaning of this ambivalence is ignored. As indicated briefly at the beginning of this chapter, Freud tended to depend on people and at the same time he was ashamed of, and hated, his dependency. After having accepted the other person's help and affection, he negated the dependency by breaking off all relations with that person, and by removing him from his life, by hating him. Freud's ardent wish for independence has been seen and emphasized by Jones, but, due partly to his idolizing tendency, and partly to the insufficiency of the orthodox theoretical construction, he overlooks the dependent aspect in Freud's character, and the conflict between the proud wish for independence and the receptive dependency.

Something very similar happened in Freud's relation-

[3] Jones, *op. cit.*, Vol. I, p. 255.

ship to Fliess. The most striking thing about this friendship, which began in 1887, is again Freud's dependency
on Fliess. During the height of this relationship, Freud
pours out to Fliess his thoughts, hopes and sorrows, and
always expects Fliess to be the concerned and interested
listener.

Here are some characteristic examples of this dependent reaction to Fliess. On January 3, 1899, Freud
writes: "I live gloomily or in darkness until you come
and then I pour out all my grumbles to you, kindle my
flickering light at your steady flame and feel well again." [4]
Or, in a letter of June 30, 1896, he writes:

> I am in a rather gloomy state, and all that I can
> say is that I am looking forward to our congress
> [Freud used this word for their meetings] as to a
> slaking of hunger and thirst. I shall bring with me
> nothing but a pair of open ears, and shall be all
> agape. Also I expect great things—so self-centered
> am I—for my own purposes. I have run into some
> doubts about my repression theory which a sug-
> gestion from you, like the one about male and female
> menstruation in the same individual, may resolve.
> Anxiety, chemical factors, etc.,—perhaps you may
> supply me with solid ground on which I shall be able
> to give up explaining things psychologically and start
> finding a firm basis in physiology.[5]

This letter is particularly interesting in the present context
because of Freud's language; that Fliess is to satisfy his

[4] *The Origins of Psychoanalysis,* p. 272.
[5] *Ibid.,* p. 169.

"hunger and thirst" is a characteristic expression of the unconscious oral-receptive dependency. It is furthermore interesting to find Freud here expressing the hope of discovering a basis for the understanding of neuroses in physiology, rather than in psychology. This hope expresses to some extent Freud's old love for physiology—but at the same time it must not be taken too seriously. Freud was not really dependent on Fliess for new ideas, although in his letter he seems to express such dependency. Freud has proved himself to be possessed by such extraordinary gifts of creativeness that we must take his conscious thoughts expressed in this letter essentially as a satisfaction of a purely emotional dependency. Freud needed somebody who would confirm him, comfort him, encourage him, listen to him and even feed him—and for years Fliess was the man to have this function.

It fits into this picture of the relationship that it is markedly one-sided, as far as interest in the other is concerned. One can hardly fail to notice that Freud, in all these years of correspondence, writes almost exclusively about himself and his ideas, and hardly at all about Fliess. There are expressions of courteous interest in Fliess's personal life, but mostly they are almost perfunctory. Freud noticed that himself, when he wrote (February 12, 1900): "I feel almost ashamed of writing to you only about myself." [6] It seems also that Fliess complained about Freud's lack of response, for we find that Freud writes in a letter of October 3, 1897: "But you must not expect an answer to everything and in the case of many of my answers you will not, I hope, fail to make allowances

[6] *Ibid.,* p. 309.

for my limitations on your subjects, which are outside my sphere." [7]

As in the case of Breuer, the break came after some years of the most intimate friendship, and the reasons for it fit into the total picture of oral-receptive ambivalence. According to Jones, "we do not exactly" know how the clash came about. "Fliess' subsequent (published) version was that Freud made a violent and unexpected attack on him, which sounds very unlikely." [8] (Considering Freud's ambivalence in his friendships, admitted by Freud and even by Jones, there seems to be nothing unlikely in it.) But whatever this attack may have been, we can see in the correspondence two very obvious reasons for the clash. One was that Fliess criticized Freud's method by saying that Freud read his own thoughts into his patients. Freud, who was never favorably disposed to accept criticism, would have accepted it least of all from the friend whose main function was to affirm, encourage and admire.

The other reason for the break is to be found in a reaction of Freud's, which again affords us an insight into his receptive strivings. Fliess's basic discovery was that of the bisexuality to be found in everyone, men and women.

At the last meeting in Achensee, in the summer of 1900, Freud announced it [the idea that all human beings had a bisexual constitution] to his friend as a new idea whereupon the astonished Fliess replied: "But I told you about that on our evening walks in Breslau [1897] and there you refused to accept the

[7] *Ibid.*, p. 278.
[8] Jones, *op. cit.*, Vol. I, p. 314.

idea." Freud had completely forgotten the talk, and denied all knowledge of it; it was only a week later that the memory of it came back to him.[9]

Jones comments in a footnote:

A severe case of amnesia! Only a year before he had written: "You are certainly right about bisexuality. I am also getting used to regarding every sexual act as one between four individuals" (August 1, 1899). And the year previous to that he had expressed his enthusiasm in the words: "I have taken to emphasizing the concept of bisexuality and I regard your idea of it as the most significant for my work since that of 'defense'" (January 4, 1898).

Jones makes no attempt to explain this "amnesia" psychoanalytically. Yet, the answer is quite clear. Freud's tendency was to receive and to swallow, and hence he tended, especially in the case of his most intimate friends, to believe that an idea was his which, as he knew only too well, was his friends'. This mechanism becomes even more illuminated if we read a letter Freud wrote to Fliess a year after this unfortunate last meeting in Achensee. In a letter of August 7, 1901, Freud states: "There is no concealing the fact that we have drawn somewhat apart from each other. By this and that I can see how much. . . . In this you came to the limit of your penetration, you take sides against me and tell me that 'the thought reader merely reads his own thoughts into other people,' which deprives my work of all its value." After thus having shown his

[9] *Ibid.*, pp. 314–15.

resentment at Fliess's critical remark, Freud makes an astonishing announcement:

> And now for the most important thing of all. My next book, as far as I can see, will be called "Bi-sexuality in Man." It will tackle the root of the problem and say the last word which it will be granted to me to say on the subject—the last and the deepest. ... The idea itself is yours. You remember my saying to you years ago, when you were still a nose specialist and surgeon, that the solution lay in sexuality. Years later you corrected me and said bisexuality, and I see that you are right. So perhaps I shall have to borrow still more from you, and perhaps I shall be compelled in honesty to ask you to add your signature to the book to mine; this would mean an expansion of the anatomic-biological part, which in my hands alone would be very meagre. I should make my aim the mental aspect of bisexuality and the explanation of the neurotic side. That, then, is the next project, which I hope will satisfactorily unite us again in scientific matters.[10]

This letter deserves detailed analysis. Why does Freud announce the book with a title which is not in the context of Freud's study in neurosis, but exactly the central point of Fliess's theory? Why does Freud, who is always modest, boast of the new book as "the last and deepest word"? Quite clearly, the answer is the same as to the questions why in 1896 he wanted with Fliess's help to find "a firm basis in physiology" and why in 1900 he had forgotten

[10] *The Origins of Psychoanalysis,* pp. 334–35.

that Fliess was the discoverer of bisexuality. He unconsciously wanted to possess his friend's discovery, not because Freud needed it, but because of the deep-seated
receptive wish to be nursed. Quite obviously, Freud in
writing the letter is aware of the conflict with Fliess, and
specifically over this matter of authorship. But he rationalizes his own claim in a subtle way. After admitting that
"the idea itself is yours," he reminds Fliess that at the
time when Fliess was "still" a nose specialist and surgeon,
he, Freud, had already discovered that "the solution lay
in sexuality," and thus Fliess's discovery is only a "correc-
tion." But even this rationalization does not seem to convince Freud himself, for he goes on to say he will be
compelled in honesty to ask Fliess to add his signature to
that of Freud's. This is not put in the form of a question,
but: "That, then, is the next project, which I hope will
satisfactorily unite us again in scientific matters." Indeed,
Freud never wrote this book, which was quite outside the
main trend of his thoughts. The whole idea was a last
attempt to force Fliess into the role of the nursing mother,
and at the same time the preparation for the complete
break, if Fliess were not ready to accept the assignment.

There follow only a few letters. Apparently Fliess criticized Freud for his plan to write *Bisexuality in Man*.
Freud answered (September 19, 1901): "I do not understand your answer about bisexuality. It is obviously very
difficult to understand one another. I certainly had no
intention of doing anything but get to grips, as my contri-
bution to the theory of bisexuality, with the thesis that
repression and the neurosis, and thus the independence of
the unconscious, presuppose bisexuality." [11] Actually,

[11] *Ibid.*, p. 377.

Freud's announcement of the book on "Bisexuality in Man" gave a quite different impression from the explanation in this letter.

There follow only a few rather impersonal letters, mostly dealing with patients whom Fliess had sent to Freud, and the last two letters which give a detailed description of how Freud was appointed professor at the University of Vienna. This communication marks the end of an eight-year-old and most intimate friendship.

A third friendship, though one much less intimate and personal than the friendships with Breuer and Fliess, was that with Jung. Here, too, we find the same development: great hopes, great enthusiasm, the break. There is one obvious difference to be seen in the relationships between Freud and Breuer, Fliess and Jung. Breuer was Freud's mentor and taught him a decisive new idea; Fliess was his equal, and Jung was his pupil. Seen superficially, these differences would be in contrast to the assumption that Freud's dependency was manifested in all three relationships. While one might admit it with regard to Breuer, or perhaps even with regard to Fliess, how can one speak of the teacher's dependency on his own pupils? Yet, seen dynamically, there is no real contradiction. There is an obvious and *conscious* dependence in which person depends on a father figure, a "magic helper," a superior, etc. But there is an *unconscious* dependence in which a dominant person is dependent on those who depend on him. In this kind of symbiotic relationship, they both depend on each other, except that the one's dependency is conscious, the other's unconscious.

This kind of dependency becomes quite clear if we consider the beginning of Freud's relationship to Jung. Freud had been greatly pleased by the fact that a group of Swiss psychiatrists, among them Bleuler, director of the Burghölzli, and his first assistant, C. G. Jung, had become actively interested in psychoanalysis. "Freud for his own part," so reports Jones, "was not only grateful for the support that had come to him from afar, but was also very attracted by Jung's personality. He soon decided that Jung was to be his successor, and at times called him 'his son and heir.' He expressed the opinion that Jung and Gross were the only true original minds among his followers. Jung was to be the Joshua destined to explore the land of psychiatry, which Freud, like Moses, was only permitted to view from afar." [12] But there was still another important angle to Freud's attitude toward Jung. So far, most of Freud's adherents had been Viennese and Jews. Freud felt it necessary for the final success of the psychoanalytic movement in the world that "Aryans" take over the leadership. He had already expressed this idea very clearly in 1908, in a letter to Karl Abraham; he rebuked Abraham for an unnecessary quarrel with Jung, and then ended the letter saying: "After all, our Aryan Comrades are quite indispensable to us; otherwise psychoanalysis would fall a victim to anti-Semitism." [13]

This conviction grew in Freud during the next two years. At the time of the Psychoanalytic Congress at Nuremberg in 1910, Freud (in a scene already referred to)

perceived the advantage of establishing a broader basis for the work than could be provided by Vien-

[12] Jones, *op. cit.*, Vol. II, pp. 32–34.
[13] Quoted by Jones, *op. cit.*, Vol. II, p. 51.

nese Jewry, and that it was necessary to convince his Viennese colleagues of this. Hearing that several of them were holding a protest meeting in Stekel's hotel room, he went up to join them, and made an impassioned appeal for their adherence. He laid stress on the virulent hostility that surrounded them, and the need for outside support to counter it. Then, dramatically throwing back his coat, he declared: "My enemies would be willing to see me starve, they would tear my very coat off my back." [14]

It was quite clear what went on in Freud's mind. His fear not only of personal starvation, but also the starvation of his psychoanalytic "movement," impelled him to see in Jung the savior from such disaster.

Freud wanted to win over Jung completely, to make him his heir and the leader of the movement. Quite characteristic of this wish is a little episode at the time of Freud's departure for the United States, together with Jung and Ferenczi. The three had dinner together, and Ferenczi together with Freud persuaded Jung to give up the principle of abstinence, and to drink a glass of wine with them. The principle of abstinence was a common bond between Jung and his teacher Bleuler and many other Swiss colleagues. The drinking of the wine was a symbol of giving up his main allegiance to Bleuler and shifting it to Freud. In fact, this change of attitude had serious after effects for the relationship between Jung and Bleuler. How deeply Freud himself experienced the symbolic meaning of this drinking ritual follows from the

[14] *Ibid.*, pp. 69–70.

fact that, immediately afterward, he fell down in a faint.[15] If there were any doubt about the psychic origin of this faint, it would be removed by the fact that Freud fainted another time at a very similar occasion.[16] During the year 1912, the relations between Freud and Jung had deteriorated. Reports came from Jung's lectures, in New York, revealing evidence of his antagonistic attitude toward Freud's theories, and toward Freud himself. Moreover, Jung had already told Freud that incest wishes were not to be taken literally, but as symbols of other tendencies. Eventually they met in Munich, in November, 1912. Freud reproached him for his tendencies of disloyalty, and Jung became "extremely contrite," accepted all the criticisms and promised to reform. At the following luncheon, Freud "began reproaching the two Swiss, Jung and Riklin, for writing articles expounding psychoanalysis in Swiss periodicals, without mentioning his name. Jung replied that they had thought it unnecessary to do so, it being so well known." [Freud] persisted, and "I remember," writes Jones, "thinking he was taking the matter rather personally. Suddenly, to our consternation, he fell on the floor in a dead faint. The sturdy Jung swiftly carried him to a couch in the lounge, where he soon revived." [17] Freud himself analyzed his reaction of fainting, and expressed the opinion that all his attacks could be traced to the effect on him of his young brother's death when he was a year and seven months old. Jones adds to this: "It would therefore seem that Freud was himself a mild case of the type he described as 'those who are

---

[15] *Ibid.,* p. 55.
[16] Cf. for the following, Jones's description, *ibid.,* pp. 143 ff.
[17] *Ibid.,* Vol. I, p. 317.

wrecked by success,' in this case the success of defeating an opponent—the earliest example of which was his successful death-wish against his little brother Julius." [18] This interpretation may be correct, but one must also consider that this fainting may be interpreted as a symbol of the child's helplessness and dependence on the motherly figure. This interpretation finds further support in the fact that years earlier, when Freud was together with his friend Fliess in the same city and the same hotel, he had fainted before. Freud describes this incident in a letter to Jones, saying: "There is some piece of unruly homosexual feeling at the root of the matter." [19] It seems much more likely that behind the faintings with Jung and with Fliess lies the same root, a deep though unconscious dependency, which finds a drastic expression in a psychosomatic symptom.

It must be added here that Freud himself was aware of such tendencies of dependency, which he called *Schnorrer* (beggar) phantasies. As one instance, he mentions that the Richettis in Paris, who liked him and had no children, provoked in him a phantasy about inheriting some of their wealth. Another such phantasy was related by Freud many years later. In this phantasy he stopped a runaway horse, and a very important person stepped out of the carriage with the words: "You are my savior—I owe my life to you! What can I do for you?" Freud's own reaction to this phantasy is quite revealing:

He promptly repressed the thoughts at the time, but years later he recovered them by the curious

[18] *Ibid.*, Vol. II, p. 146.
[19] *Ibid.*, Vol. I, p. 317.

route of finding he was attributing them in error to a supposed story by Alphonse Daudet. It was an annoying recollection, since by then he had got over his earlier need for a patronage, and would violently repudiate it. "But the provoking part of it all [wrote Freud] *is the fact that there is scarcely anything to which I am so hostile as the thought of being some one's protégé.* What we see of that sort of thing in our country spoils all desire for it, and my character is little suited to the role of a protected child. I have always entertained a strong desire to be a strong man myself." [20]

This is one of Freud's curiously naïve statements, so clearly a sign of resistance, and yet taken quite seriously by himself. This was exactly his conflict; he desired to be independent; he hated to be a protégé—and at the same time he wanted to be protected, admired, cared for—and he never solved this conflict.

To come back to Freud's friendship with Jung, it took the same course as his relationship with Breuer and Fliess. In spite of Jung's repeated assertions of loyalty, both personal relations and scientific views became more and more estranged, until it came to the final and irrevocable break in 1914. Doubtless this was a severe blow for Freud; here again he had depended on a man, to whom he had opened his heart about his own worries and hopes, and whom he visualized as the one who would guarantee the future of the movement, and again he had to break up the relationship. There is one difference, however, between

[20] *Ibid.,* pp. 188–89. (Italics mine. E. F.)

the break with Jung and those with Breuer, Fliess, Adler, Stekel, Rank and Ferenczi, inasmuch as the scientific differences with Jung were more basic than with the others. Freud was a rationalist, and his concern with the understanding of the unconscious was based on his wish to control and to subdue it. Jung, on the other hand, belonged to the romantic, antirationalistic tradition. He is suspicious of reason and intellect, and the unconscious, representing the non-rational, to him is the deepest source of wisdom; for him, analytic therapy has the function of helping the patient to get in touch with this source of non-rational wisdom, and to benefit from this contact. Jung's interest in the unconscious was the admiring one of the romantic; Freud's, the critical one of the rationalist. They could meet for a while in passing, but going in different directions; the break was unavoidable.

Freud's relationship to some of the others on whom he had relied most, especially on Adler, Rank and Ferenczi, followed the same path we have seen in his relationship to Breuer, Fliess and Jung: ardent friendship, confidence, dependence changing sooner or later into suspiciousness and hate. Some of these relationships will be discussed later on.

V.

His Relationship to His Father

FREUD'S *relationship to his father* was exactly the opposite of that to his mother. She admired him and indulged him, permitting him to be the king among his siblings—his father was apparently a more impartial though unaggressive man. Characteristic of this difference is the fact that when at the age of two he was still wetting his bed, it was his father, and not his mother, who reproved him. And what did the little boy answer? "Don't worry, Papa, I will buy you a beautiful new red bed in Neutitschein." [1] We see here already the traits which would characterize Freud in his later life: a difficulty in accepting criticism, a supreme self-confidence, and rebelliousness against his father and, as we may also say, fatherly authority. He, at the age of two, is not impressed by his father's scolding, but puts himself into the shoes of the father, as one who can make him a gift of the bed later. (Cf. the earlier dream about the Turkish coat, pp. 10–11.)

[1] Quoted from Jones, *op. cit.*, Vol. I, p. 7.

A more drastic expression of his rebelliousness toward his father is to be found in the fact, that at the age of seven or eight, he deliberately urinated in the bedroom of his parents. This was a symbolic act of taking possession of his parents' bedroom, with an aggressive tendency, obviously directed against his father. His father reacted, quite understandably, with anger, and exclaimed: "That boy will never amount to anything." Freud, in commenting on this incident, wrote: "This must have been a terrible affront to my ambition, for allusions to this scene occur again and again in my dreams and are constantly coupled with enumerations of my accomplishments and success, as if I wanted to say: 'You see I have amounted to something after all.' "[2]

This explanation given by Freud that his father's remark was the *cause* of his ambition is an error which one can find frequently in orthodox analytic interpretations. While it is, of course, true that early experiences are one of the most important causes of later development, it is also not rare that the child's—acquired or inherited—disposition can *provoke* a reaction in the parent, which then is often erroneously taken for the *cause* of the development of this very disposition in the child's later life.

In this case it is clear that the little Freud, at the age of two, had already a sense of importance and of superiority toward his father. Whether we deal here with a constitutional factor or with the results of the fact that his mother was the stronger one in the family, his provocative act at the age of seven was only one *more* expression of the little boy's supreme self-confidence, which was to be continued

[2] Sigmund Freud, *The Interpretation of Dreams,* p. 216.

throughout his whole life, while his father's remark was a mild reaction of a very unaggressive man who, as Jones asserts, was usually very proud of his son and not in the habit of criticizing or belittling him. This one—and rather isolated—remark cannot possibly have been the cause of Freud's ambitiousness.

Freud's superior attitude to his father must have received new stimulation from a story his father told him when he was a boy of twelve. When he (the father) was a young man, a Gentile had knocked off his fur cap, and then shouted at him: "Jew, get off the pavement!" When the little boy asked indignantly, "And what did you do?" his father replied: "I went into the roadway and picked up my cap." Freud, in relating this story, continued: "This struck me as unheroic conduct on the part of the big strong man who was holding the little boy by the hand. I contrasted this situation with another which fitted my feelings better: the scene in which Hannibal's father, Hamilcar Barca, made his boy swear before the household altar to take vengeance on the Romans. Ever since that time, Hannibal had a place in my phantasies."[3] It should be clear that the story of his father's unheroic reaction would not have created such resentment in Freud had it not been for the fact that Freud had identified himself with the hero Hannibal since his childhood; he wanted a father worthy of himself. But we must not forget that Freud's ambition was, as ambitions so often are, part and parcel of his own outstanding gifts—his indomitable courage and pride. This courage gave Freud, even the little boy, the quality—and the ideal—of the hero, and

[3] *Ibid.*, p. 197.

the hero could not help being ashamed of his unheroic father.

Freud himself hints at this resentment that his father was not a greater man in the following interpretation of one of his own dreams:

> The fact [Freud writes] that in this scene of my dream I can use my father to screen Meynert [professor of psychiatry at Vienna University] is explained not by any discovered analogy between the two persons, but by the fact that it is the brief but perfectly adequate representation of a conditional sentence in the dream thoughts, which, if fully expanded, would read as follows: "Of course, if I belonged to the second generation, if I were the son of a professor or a privy councillor, I should have progressed more rapidly." In my dream I make my father a professor and a privy councillor.[4]

Freud's ambivalence to the father figure is also reflected in his theoretical work. In his construction of the beginning of human history in *Totem and Tabu,* he has the primordial father slain by the jealous sons; in his last work, *Moses and Monotheism,* he denies that Moses was a Jew and makes him out to be the son of an Egyptian nobleman, thus saying unconsciously: "Just as Moses was not born from humble Jews, I am also not a Jew but a man of royal descent." [5] The most significant expression of Freud's own ambivalent attitude toward his father

[4] *Ibid.,* p. 438.
[5] The same thought has been expressed by H. W. Puner, *op. cit.,* p. 180.

may, of course, be seen in one of the central concepts of his whole system, the concept of the Oedipus complex: the son hating his father as his rival for Mother's love. But here as in the case of the attachment to Mother, the sexual interpretation of this rivalry obscures the real and fundamental reasons. The wish for unlimited love and admiration by Mother, and, at the same time, the aspiration to be the conquering hero, lead to the claim of supremacy with regard to both Father and siblings. (This constellation is presented most clearly in the biblical story of Joseph and his brothers. One might be tempted to call this complex the "Joseph complex.") This attitude is often furthered by the mother's own worshiping attitude toward the son, in connection with her ambivalent, belittling attitude toward the husband.

What do we find, then? Freud was deeply attached to his mother, convinced of her love and admiration, and felt himself to be the superior, unique, admirable person, the king among all other sons and daughters. He remained dependent on motherly help and admiration—and felt worried, anxious and depressed when it was not forthcoming. While his mother remained a central figure in his life until her death in her nineties, and while his wife had to fulfill a motherly function, taking care of his material needs, his need for admiration and protection he turned to new objects, and mainly to men rather than to women. People like Breuer, Fliess, Jung and, later on, his faithful disciples, gave him the kind of admiration and affirmation which Freud needed in order to be secure. As is so often the case with mother-attached men, his father was his rival; *he,* the son, wanted to be the father himself, the hero. Maybe if his father had been the great man himself, Freud might have submitted to him, or have been less rebellious. But Freud, identifying himself with the heroes, had to rebel against a father who would only have been good enough for an ordinary son.

Freud's rebellious attitude toward his father touches upon one of the most important aspects of Freud's personality as far as his work is concerned. Freud is generally considered to have been a rebel. He defied public opinion and medical authorities, and without the capacity for such defiance, he could never have held and proclaimed his views on the unconscious, infantile sexuality, etc. Yet Freud was a *rebel* and not a *revolutionary*. By rebel I refer to a person who fights existing authorities, but who himself wants to be an authority (to whom others submit), and who does not dissolve his dependence on and respect for authority per se. His rebelliousness is directed mainly against those authorities who do not acknowledge him, and he is friendly to those authorities who are of his own choosing, especially when he becomes one of them. The type of the "rebel," in this psychological sense, can be found among many radical politicians who are rebels before they have power, and turn conservative once they have acquired power for themselves. A "revolutionary" in the psychological sense is someone who overcomes his ambivalence toward authority because he frees himself from attachment to authority and from the wish to dominate others. He achieves true independence and he overcomes the yearning for domination of others. In this psychological sense, Freud was a rebel, and not a revolutionary. While he defied authorities and enjoyed this defiance, he was at the same time deeply impressed by the existing social order and its authorities. To receive the title of a professor, and to find recognition from the existing authorities, were of utmost concern to him, although in a strange unawareness of his own desires he denied it; [6] in the First World War he was a fiery patriot, proud first of Austrian, then of German aggressiveness, and for almost four years it never dawned on him to question critically the war ideologies and goals of the central powers.

[6] Cf. *The Interpretation of Dreams*, p. 192.

VI.

Freud's Authoritarianism

THE problem of Freud's authoritarianism has been the subject of a great deal of discussion. It has been maintained frequently that Freud was of a rigid authoritarianism and thus intolerant of other opinions or revisions of his own theories. It is hard to ignore the bulk of evidence which supports this view. Freud never accepted any significant suggestions for change in his theoretical work. Either one had to be completely in favor of his theory—and that meant of *him*—or one was against him. Even Sachs, in his frankly idolizing biography of Freud, admits this: "I knew it was always extremely difficult for him to assimilate the opinions of others after he had evolved his own in a long and laborious process." [1] And as to his own digression from Freud, Sachs writes: "If my opinion was opposed to his, I said so frankly. He always gave me full scope to expound my views, and listened willingly to my arguments, but *was hardly ever moved by them.*" [2]

[1] Hanns Sachs, *Freud, Master and Friend,* Harvard University Press, Cambridge, 1946, p. 14.
[2] *Ibid.,* p. 13. (My italics. E. F.)

The most drastic example of Freud's intolerance and authoritarianism can be found in his relationship to Ferenczi. Ferenczi, who for many years had been the most loyal, unpretentious pupil and friend, toward the end of his life suggested that the patient needs love, the love which he had needed and not received as a child. This led to a certain change in technique, away from the completely impersonal and mirror-like attitude which Freud had proposed, to a human and loving attitude toward the patient. (Needless to say, by loving, Ferenczi meant motherly, or motherly-fatherly love, not erotic or sexual love.)

"When I visited the Professor," so reported Ferenczi in a conversation with a trusted friend and disciple,

I told him of my latest technical ideas. These are empirically based on my work with my patients. I have tried to discover from my patients' told history, from their association of ideas, from the way they behave—even in detailed respects and especially toward me—from the frustrations which arouse their anger or depression, and especially from the content —both conscious and unconscious—of their desires and longings, the manner in which they suffered rejection at the hands of their mothers or their parents or surrogates. And I have also endeavored through empathy to imagine what kind of loving care, even in specific details of behavior, the patient really needed at that early age—a loving care and nurture which would have allowed his self-confidence, his self-enjoyment, to develop wholesomely. Each patient needs a different experience of tender, supporting care. It is not easy to discern this, for it is usually not what he consciously believes it to be—often quite different. It is possible to sense when I am on the right track; for the patient immediately unconsciously gives the signal by a number of slight changes in mood and behavior. Even his dreams show a response to the new and beneficent treatment. All this should be confided to the patient—the analyst's new understanding of his needs, his ensuing change of relationship to the patient and his expression of this, and the patient's own evident response. Whenever mistakes are made by the analyst, the patient again gives the signal by becoming angry or despondent. And his dreams make clear the analyst's errors. All this can be elicited from the patient and explained to him. The analyst must then continue his search for the beneficent treatment, so deeply needed by his patient. This process is one of trial and error with eventual success, and must be pursued by the analyst with all skill and tact and loving-kindness, and fearlessly. It must be absolutely honest and genuine.

The Professor listened to my exposition with increasing impatience and finally warned me that I was treading on dangerous ground and was departing fundamentally from the traditional customs and techniques of Psychoanalysis. Such yielding to the patient's longings and desires—no matter how genuine—would increase his dependence on the analyst. Such dependence can only be destroyed by the emotional withdrawal of the analyst. In the hands of unskilled analysts my method, the Professor said, might easily lead to sexual indulgence rather than be an expression of parental devotion.

This warning ended the interview. I held out my hand in affectionate adieu. The Professor turned his back on me and walked out of the room.[3]

Another expression of Freud's intolerance is his attitude toward those members of the International Association who were not completely loyal to the party line. Characteristic is a sentence in a letter to Jones (February 18, 1919), in which Freud says: "Your intention to *purge* the London Society of the Jungian members is excellent." [4]

The same spirit of Freud's unforgiving attitude toward dissenting friends is to be found in his reaction to Alfred Adler's death. In an answer to Arnold Zweig, who had expressed how moved he was by Adler's death, Freud wrote: "I don't understand your sympathy for Adler. For a Jew-boy out of a Viennese suburb a death in Aberdeen is an unheard-of career in itself, and a proof of how far he had got on. The world really rewarded him richly

[3] Personal communication from Izette de Forest, student and friend of Ferenczi, and author of *The Leaven of Love* (Harper & Brothers, New York, 1954), which contains an excellent exposition of Ferenczi's new ideas.

Freud's intolerance toward Ferenczi's new ideas was also expressed in the fact that he wanted him to promise not to publish the paper he was to give at the congress in Wiesbaden. This paper has been published under the title "Confusion of Tongues" in Volume III of the *Collected Papers* by Ferenczi (ed. by Clara Thompson, Basic Books, Inc.). As anybody who reads it can convince himself, it is a paper of extraordinary profundity and brilliance—one of the most valuable papers in the whole psychoanalytic literature; it contains, however, certain important though subtle deviations from Freud's thought.

[4] Quoted by Jones, *op. cit.,* Vol. II, p. 254. (My italics. E. F.)

for his service in having contradicted psychoanalysis." [5]

In spite of all this evidence, the faithful worshipers of Freud make it a point to deny any authoritarian tendency in Freud. Jones makes this point again and again. Thus, for instance, he says people tell "of Freud's tyrannical personality and his dogmatic insistence on each of his followers accepting precisely the same views as himself. That such accusations are ridiculously untrue is clear from his correspondence, his writing and, above all, from the memories of those who worked with him." [6] Or: "Anyone temperamentally less fitted to resemble the dictator he has at times been depicted as being, I should find it hard to imagine." [7]

Jones is of a psychological naïveté in these assertions which ill fit a psychoanalyst. He simply overlooks the fact that Freud was intolerant to those who questioned or criticized him in the least. To people who idolized him and never disagreed, he was kind and tolerant; just because, as I have emphasized before, Freud was so dependent on unconditional affirmation and agreement by others, he was a loving father to submissive sons, and a stern, authoritarian one to those who dared to disagree.

Sachs is more frank than Jones. While Jones believes that he gives an objective picture, as a biographer should, Sachs frankly admits his "thorough lack of objectivity, which I profess freely and cheerfully. . . . On the whole, idolizing, if it is perfectly genuine, will add to the truth-

[5] Letter to A. Zweig, June 22, 1936, quoted by Jones, *op. cit.*, Vol. III, p. 208.
[6] *Ibid.*, Vol. II, pp. 127–28.
[7] *Ibid.*, p. 129.

fulness rather than stand in its way." [8] How far the symbiotic, quasi-religious attachment to Freud went follows
from Sachs's statement that when he had finished reading Freud's *Interpretation of Dreams,* "I had found the
one thing worth while for me to live for; many years
later I discovered that it was also the only thing I could
live by." [9] We can easily imagine somebody saying that
he lives by the Bible, the Bhagavad-Gita, or by the
philosophy of Spinoza or Kant—but to live by a book
on the interpretation of dreams makes sense only if we
assume that the author has become a Moses and the
science a new religion. That Sachs never rebelled against
or criticized Freud becomes pathetically evident from
his own description of the one occasion where Sachs
"willfully and persistently" did something of which Freud
disapproved. "He spoke to me about it when it was
almost over, only three or four words, in a low voice,
nearly as an aside. These words, the only unfriendly ones
I ever heard from him, remain deeply graven in my
memory. However, when this episode was over, it was
forgiven if not forgotten, and it had no lasting influence
on his attitude toward me. If I cannot now think of it
without feeling a bit ashamed, this feeling is tempered
by the thought: only once in a life-time, once in thirty-
five years. That is not such a bad record." [10]

[8] Sachs, *op. cit.,* pp. 8–9.
[9] *Ibid.,* pp. 3–4.
[10] *Ibid.,* pp. 16–17.

VII.

Freud, the World Reformer

FREUD was a child with a marked admiration for great military leaders. The great Carthaginian Hannibal and Napoleon's allegedly Jewish general Masséna, were his earliest heroes.[1] He was passionately interested in the Napoleonic Wars, and pasted the names of Napoleon's marshals on the backs of his wooden soldiers. At the age of fourteen, he became very interested in the Franco-Prussian War. He had maps with little flags in his studio, and discussed problems of strategy with his sisters.[2] These enthusiasms and interests have a double aspect: one is the interest in history and politics; the other is the enthusiasm for the great leader who influences history and transforms the fate of mankind. That Freud's enthusiasm for Hannibal and Masséna and his interest in the Franco-Prussian War were motivated by his concern for history and political progress—and were not simply the boy's passion for uniforms and battles—is borne out by the further development of Freud's political interest. When

---

[1] Jones, *op. cit.*, Vol. I, p. 8.
[2] *Ibid.*, p. 23.

he was about seventeen, he seriously thought of studying law; this was the time of the "bourgeois ministry."

> Shortly before, my father [so Freud reports] had brought home portraits of these middle class professional men—Herbst, Giska, Unger, Gerger, and others—and we had illuminated the house in their honor. There had even been some Jews among them; so henceforth every industrious Jewish schoolboy carried a cabinet minister's portfolio in his satchel. The events of that period no doubt had some bearing on the fact that up to the time shortly before I entered the University it had been my intention to study law; it was only in the last moment that I changed my mind.[3]

This idea of the seventeen-year-old Freud of becoming a political leader is confirmed by his school friendship with Heinrich Braun, who was Freud's classmate, and who was to become later one of the leading German socialists. Freud himself describes this friendship many years later in a letter to Heinrich Braun's widow.

> In the Gymnasium [Freud writes] we were inseparable friends. . . . All the hours of the day which were left after school I spent with him. . . . Neither the goals nor the means for our ambitions were very clear to us. Since then I have come to the assumption that his aims were essentially negative ones. *But one thing was certain: that I would work with him and that I could never desert his party.* Under his in-

---

[3] *The Interpretation of Dreams*, p. 193.

fluence I was also determined at that time to study law at the university.[4]

In view of this probable interest in socialism in late adolescence, it is no surprise to find an unconscious act of identification with Victor Adler, the admired leader of the Austrian Social Democratic party. Mrs. S. Bernfeld has drawn attention to this fact in a discussion of the circumstances under which Freud rented his apartment in the Berggasse. Until 1891, Freud, with his family, had lived in the Schottenring; one child was on the way, and the family had decided to move.

The move was carefully planned by both Professor and Mrs. Freud. They made lists of their most important requirements. They spent a considerable time planning their new home. . . . One afternoon after he [Freud] had finished his calls he went for a walk. After enjoying the many gardens that he passed he found himself in front of a house that had a sign "For Rent." He suddenly experienced a great attraction to this house. He walked in, looked at the apartment that was opened to him, found that it fulfilled all his requirements and immediately signed the lease. This house was Berggasse 19. He went home, told his wife that he found the ideal place for them and took her that same evening to look at it. Mrs. Freud saw all its faults. However, with characteristic intuition Mrs. Freud realized that Freud

[4] Letter to Julie Braun-Vogelstern, published and discussed by M. Grotjahn in the *Journal of the American Psychoanalytic Association*, Vol. IV, October, 1956, p. 644. (Italics mine. E. F.)

had to have this house and no other house would
do. So she said that she liked it and that she thought
they would be able to manage. They did manage
and lived in this gloomy and impractical house for
forty-seven years.[5]

"What could lead," asked Mrs. Bernfeld, "so careful and
thoughtful a man as Freud to such an impulsive and
inconsiderate act and what could keep him for so many
years in this house?" [6] The answer given by Mrs. Bernfeld to this very justified question points to the fact that
Victor Adler, the ardent socialist and later the undisputed leader of Austrian socialism, had lived in this same
apartment and that Freud, who had been invited to Adler's home years before, had been greatly impressed by
the household of this man. Some slips with regard to the
dates concerning the house are also interpreted by the
author as indicating the importance of the connection
with Adler. While I entirely agree with Mrs. Bernfeld's
suggestion, I believe she misses one point which is important in the present context: Freud's humanitarian
ideals and his own ambition to become a great political
leader.

There is still another socialist leader with whom Freud
must have identified himself. This seems to be indicated
by the fact that the motto which Freud gave *The Interpretation of Dreams* ("*Flectere si nequeo superos, Acheronta movebo,*" [7] from Virgil, *Aeneas*, VII, 32) was used
by the great German socialist leader Lasalle in his book
Der italienische Krieg und die Aufgabe Preussens, 1859.

[5] *Ibid.*, p. 650.
[6] *Ibid.*

Freud was using the same motto under the influence of Lasalle. The proof seems to be found in Freud's letter to Fliess (July 17, 1899), where he writes: "In addition to my manuscript I am taking the 'Lasalle' and a few works on the unconscious to Berchtesgaden. . . . New introductory quotation for the dreams has suggested itself since you condemned the sentimental one from Goethe. It will have to be just a hint at repression. Flectere si nequeo superos Acheronta movebo." [8] It would be curious if, in view of the fact that Lasalle used this very motto in one of his books, the book mentioned in this letter had not been the one containing the motto. The fact that Freud does not write explicitly that he is using Lasalle's motto would point to the unconscious character of the identification with this socialist leader.

Before I speak in greater detail of other identifications I want to mention some further facts which show how deeply Freud was concerned, not with medicine, but with philosophy, politics and ethics. Jones reports that in 1910 Freud was expressing "the wish with a sigh that he could retire from medical practice and devote himself to the unravelling of cultural and historical problems —ultimately the great problem of how man came to be what he is." [9] Or as Freud puts it himself: "In my youth I felt an overpowering need to understand something of the riddles of the world in which we live and perhaps even to contribute something to their solution." [10]

[7] "If I cannot bend the heavens, I'll move Hell."

[8] *The Origins of Psychoanalysis,* p. 286. I owe this suggestion about the motto's connection with Lasalle and the proof in this letter to a personal communication from Professor Ernst Simon.

[9] Jones, *op. cit.,* Vol. I, p. 27.

[10] *Ibid.,* p. 28.

It is in line with this humanitarian political interest that, in 1910, Freud became interested in joining an "International Fraternity for Ethics and Culture," which had been founded by an apothecary, Knapp, and of which Forel was president. Freud advised Knapp to discuss the matter with Jung and asked Jung's opinion about the advisability of joining them. Freud wrote: "What attracted me was the practical, aggressive as much as protective feature of the program: the obligation to fight directly against the authority of the state and the Church in cases where they are committing manifest injustice." [11] Nothing came of this scheme and as Jones says, "It was soon displaced by the formation of a purely psychoanalytical association." While Freud's idea of joining the International Fraternity shows how alive still in 1910 the older ideals of progressive world improvement were in him, once he had organized the psychoanalytic movement, his overt interest in ethical culture, etc., disappeared and was transformed, as I shall try to show, into the aims of the Movement. Freud saw himself as its leader and in this role identified himself unconsciously with his earlier hero, Hannibal, and with Moses, the great leader of his own ancestors.

"Hannibal," he reports,

had been the favorite hero of my later school days. Like so many boys of that age, I had sympathized in the Punic Wars, not with the Romans, but with the Carthaginians. And when in the higher classes, I began to understand for the first time what it meant

[11] *Ibid.*, Vol. II, p. 68 (Freud's letter to Jung, January 13, 1910).

to belong to an alien race, and anti-semitic feelings among the other boys warned me that I must take up a definite position, the figure of the semitic general rose still higher in my esteem. . . . And the wish to go to Rome had become in my dream life a cloak and symbol for a number of other passionate wishes. Their realization was to be pursued with all the perseverance and single-mindedness of the Carthaginian, though this fulfillment seemed at the moment as little favored by destiny as was Hannibal's lifelong wish to enter Rome.[12]

Freud's identification with Hannibal lasted long beyond his adolescence. As a grown-up man he had a craving to go to Rome, about the irrational nature of which he wrote in a letter to Fliess (December 3, 1897). "Incidentally," he writes, "my longing for Rome is deeply neurotic. It is connected with my school-boy hero worship of the Semitic Hannibal, and in fact this year I have no more reached Rome, than he did from Lake Trasimeno."[13] Indeed, Freud avoided for years going to Rome when he was in Italy. On one of his journeys to Italy he came to Lake Trasimeno and, finally, after having seen the Tiber, he sadly turned back when he was only fifty miles from Rome.[14] He then made a plan for a visit to Italy the following year, only to by-pass Rome again. It was not until 1901 that he permitted himself to go there.

What was the reason for this strange hesitancy to

[12] *The Interpretation of Dreams,* pp. 196–97.
[13] *The Origins of Psychoanalysis,* p. 141.
[14] Cf. *The Interpretation of Dreams,* p. 196.

reach Rome, which he had been longing to see for years?
He thought that the reason was that "at the season of
the year when it is possible for me to travel, residence in
Rome must be avoided for reasons of health." [15] Yet,
Freud writes in 1909 that "it took only a little courage"
to fulfill his wish and that thereafter he became a constant pilgrim to Rome.[16] Quite obviously the "reason" of
the danger to health was a rationalization. What was it
then that made Freud avoid Rome? The only plausible
reason for Freud's inhibition to visit Rome can be found
in his unconscious.

Visiting Rome meant, apparently, for Freud's unconscious, the conquest of the enemy city, the conquest of
the world. Rome was Hannibal's aim, it was Napoleon's
aim, and it was the capital of the Catholic Church, which
Freud deeply disliked. In his identification with Hannibal, he could not go further than his hero until, years
later, he made the final step and entered Rome; quite
evidently a symbolic victory and self-affirmation, after the
appearance of his *chef-d'oeuvre, The Interpretation of
Dreams*.

There was another identification which contributed to
his not reaching Rome for so many years—the identification with Moses. He dreamt: ". . . . someone led me to
the top of the hill and showed me Rome half shrouded
in mist; it was so far away that I was surprised at my
view being so clear; but the theme of the 'promised land
seen from afar' was obvious in it." [17]

Freud himself felt this identification, partly conscious-

15 *Ibid.*, p. 194.
16 See footnote, *ibid.*
17 *Ibid.*, p. 194.

ly, partly unconsciously. His conscious idea was expressed in letters to Jung (February 28, 1908, and January 17, 1909). Declaring that Jung and Otto Gross were the only truly original minds among his followers, he wrote that Jung was to be the Joshua destined to explore the promised land of psychiatry, which Freud, like Moses, was only permitted to view from afar.[18] Jones adds that "this remark is of interest as indicating Freud's self identification with Moses, one which in later years became very evident."

Freud's unconscious identification with Moses is expressed in two of his works, in "The Moses of Michelangelo" (1914) and in his last book, *Moses and Monotheism.* "The Moses of Michelangelo" is unique in all of Freud's writings, inasmuch as it is the only paper which he published anonymously in *Imago* (Vol. III, 1914). The paper was prefaced by the following editorial note:

Although this paper does not, strictly speaking, conform to the conditions under which contributions are accepted for publication in this Journal, the editors have decided to print it, since the author who is personally known to them, belongs to psychoanalytic circles, and since his mode of thought has in point of fact a certain resemblance to the methodology of psychoanalysis.

Why did Freud write this paper, in which he does not use the psychoanalytic method, and why did he have to hide behind this anonymity, when it would have been

[18] Jones, *op. cit.*, Vol. II, p. 33.

quite feasible to publish the paper with a remark that since it was Freud's, it was published even though it was not strictly psychoanalytic? The answer to both questions must lie in the fact that the Moses figure was of great emotional importance to Freud, yet an importance which was not clearly recognized consciously, and against the recognition of which must have existed a considerable resistance.

What is the main result of Freud's minute examination of Michelangelo's statue? He suggests that this statue describes Moses not, as most observers have assumed, before having smashed the tablets of the law in a fit of rage, but, on the contrary, Freud tries to prove in an ingenious and painstaking way that Michelangelo has, in this sculpture, made an alteration in the character of Moses. "The Moses of legend and tradition had a hasty temper and was subject to fits of passion. . . . But Michelangelo has placed a different Moses on the tomb of the Pope, one superior to the historical or traditional Moses." Thus, according to Freud, Michelangelo has modified the theme of the broken tablets; he does not have Moses break them but has him calm his wrath, out of concern and compassion for the people. In this way he has added something new and more than human to the figure of Moses; so that "the giant frame with its tremendous physical power becomes only a concrete expression of the highest mental achievement that is possible in a man, that of struggling successfully against an inward passion for the sake of a cause to which he has devoted himself." [19] If one considers that this was written around

[19] Freud, *Collected Papers,* Vol. IV, p. 283.

the time of Jung's desertion, if one remembers further-more how Freud considered himself a part of the elite characterized by the ability to control their passions, then there remains little doubt that Freud was so passionately interested in his interpretation of the Moses sculpture because he saw himself as Moses, not understood by the people and yet able to control his wrath and to continue his work. This assumption is further supported by Freud's reaction to the efforts of Jones and Ferenczi to have him publish the paper under his name. "The reasons he gave for his decision," reports Jones, "seem rather thin. 'Why disgrace Moses,' said Freud, 'by putting my name to it? It is a joke but perhaps not a bad one.' " [20] On the face of it the idea that Moses would be disgraced by putting Freud's name to the article about him does not make much sense. This remark, however, makes a lot of sense if one considers it as the embarrassed reaction to the unconscious identification with Moses, which was the motive power behind the article.

How important the Moses theme was for Freud is demonstrated further by the fact that he devoted much time in the last years of his life to the person of Moses. During the time of the Hitler rule (the first and second parts of the Moses book were published in 1937, the third in 1939), Freud tried to prove that Moses had not been a Hebrew but an Egyptian. What could have prompted Freud to deprive the Jews of their greatest hero at the very time when a powerful barbarian was trying to ex-tinguish them? What could provoke Freud to write a book, far away from his field, and to try to prove some-

[20] Jones, *op. cit.,* Vol. II, p. 366.

thing on the evidence of analogies and rather thin reasoning? One answer seems certain: that the motive behind the writing of this book was the same fascination and identification with Moses which had given rise to his paper on Michelangelo over twenty years earlier. This time, it seems, it was not "a joke," and Freud was not afraid to give a bad name to Moses by putting his name to that of the hero. But he did something, not against Moses, but against the Jews: he deprived them not only of their hero, but also of the claim to the originality of the monotheistic idea.[21] If this had been Freud's field, or if his proof had been overwhelming, no psychological questions need be asked as to the motive of Freud's publication of *Moses and Monotheism*. But since this is not so, one must assume that Freud's preoccupation with Moses was rooted in the deep unconscious identification with him. Freud, like the great leader of the Jews, had led the people to the promised land, without reaching it himself; he had experienced their ingratitude and scorn, without giving up his mission.

Another identification, aside from those with Hannibal and Moses, although one of much less weight, may be mentioned, that with Columbus. After Jung left the movement Freud remarked: "Does one know today with whom Columbus sailed when he discovered America?"[22] Eventually, toward the end of his life, a dream of Freud's shows how deeply rooted this identification with a vic-

---

[21] E. Simon, in his paper on "S. Freud, the Jew" (p. 289) has pointed out the significance of the fact that Freud (in the third essay) speaks of the possibility that monotheism may originally perhaps have come to Egypt from the Near or Far East, or even from Palestine.

[22] E. Jones, *op. cit.*, Vol. II, p. 127.

torious hero was. When Freud was on the train which brought him from Paris to London on his flight from Vienna, he dreamed that he was landing at Pevensey where William the Conqueror had landed in 1066.[23] What marvelous expression of pride and confidence by a man whom nothing could break. At the end of his life, arriving in England as an old, sick refugee, his unconscious felt that he was arriving in this land of refuge as the hero and conqueror.

In view of the obvious continuity in Freud's identification with great leaders, from Napoleon's marshals to Hannibal and Moses, it is amazing indeed to find that Jones assumes that they disappeared after Freud's adolescence. "But what is significant," says Jones, "is the extraordinary change that must have set in at about the age of sixteen or seventeen. Gone is the pugnacious child who fought vigorously with his playfellows, the boy full of military ardor, the youth who dreamed of becoming a Cabinet Minister and ruling the nation. Was, after all, the two days' encounter with a country girl so very fateful?"[24]

No, indeed, this encounter was not so fateful (a case of the young Freud being enamoured of a girl for a short time). Nothing else was fateful either in this respect, since Jones is simply mistaken in the assumption that all these youthful phantasies and desires had gone. They had simply taken new forms, and partly they were less conscious. The boy who wanted to become a Cabinet Minister had become one who aspired to be like Moses, bringing a new knowledge to the human race, a knowl-

[23] Cf. Jones, *op. cit.*, Vol. III, p. 228.
[24] *Ibid.*, Vol. I, p. 53.

edge which was the last word in man's understanding of himself and of the world. Not nationalism, not socialism, not religion could be trusted as guides to a better life; the full understanding of man's mind could show the irrationality of all these answers and could lead man as far as he was destined to go: to a sober, skeptical, rational appraisal of his past and his present, and to the acceptance of the fundamentally tragic nature of his existence.

Freud saw himself as the leader of this intellectual revolution, which made the last step rationalism could make. Only if one understands this aspiration of Freud to bring a new message to mankind, not a happy but a realistic one, can one understand his creation: *the psychoanalytic movement*.

What a strange phenomenon, this psychoanalytic movement! Psychoanalysis is a therapy, that of neurosis, and it is at the same time a psychological theory, a general theory of human nature and specifically of the existence of the unconscious and its manifestations in dreams, symptoms, in character and in all symbolic productions. Is there any other case of a therapy or of a scientific theory transforming itself into a movement, centrally directed by a secret committee, with purges of deviant members, with local organizations in an international superorganization? No therapy in the field of medicine was ever transformed into such a movement. As far as psychoanalysis as a theory is concerned, the nearest comparison would be Darwinism; here is a revolutionary theory, shedding light on the history of man, and tending to change his picture of the world more fundamentally than any other theory in the nineteenth century—yet there is no Darwinian "movement," no directorium which leads that movement, no purges which decide who has the right to call himself a Darwinist and who has lost such a privilege.

Why this unique role of the psychoanalytic movement? The answer lies partly in the foregoing analysis of Freud's personality. He was a great scientist indeed; but like Marx, who was a great sociologist and economist, Freud had still another aim, one that a man like Darwin did not have: he wanted to transform the world. Under the disguise of a therapist and a scientist he was one of the great world reformers of the beginning twentieth century.

VIII.

The Quasi-Political Character of the Psychoanalytic Movement

IN THE following pages I shall try to show the peculiar quasi-political character of the psychoanalytic movement. I could hardly find a better introduction to this topic than to quote the table of contents of the first part of the third volume of Jones's biography, entitled *Life*. The subheadings of this part are: Emergence from Isolation (1901–1906); The Beginning of International Recognition (1906–1909); The International Psychoanalytic Association, Opposition, Dissensions (1911–1914); The Committee; The War-Years (1914–1919); Reunion, Discussion, Progress and Misfortune; Fame and Suffering; Last Years in Vienna; London—The End.

Anyone reading these headings would hardly doubt that the book deals with the history of a political or a religious movement, its growth and its schisms; that this is the history of a therapy, or a psychological theory, would be a most unexpected surprise. Yet, this spirit of a world-conquering movement already existed in the early years of psychoanalysis. Before 1910, Freud had made his most fundamental discoveries and presented them in a number of books and papers to a small group of physicians and psychologists in Vienna. So far, his activities had not been different from those of any other creative scientist. But this kind of activity was unsatisfactory for Freud. Between 1910 and 1914 "was launched," as Jones puts it, "what was called the 'Psychoanalytic Movement,' not a very happy phrase, but one employed by friends and foes alike." These years of

> the enjoyment of the increasing success and recognition were greatly impaired by the sinister signs of forming dissension among valued adherents. . . . Freud was immensely troubled and also bewildered by the insoluble problems this gave rise to and the perplexity of coping with them. We shall, however, confine ourselves here to the brighter side of the story, the gradual diffusion of the new ideas that naturally meant so much to Freud.[1]

I have already mentioned that Freud, shortly before he founded the "movement," wrote to Jung saying he was playing with the idea of getting his supporters to join "some larger group working for a practical idea." [2] He thought that the International Fraternity for Ethics and Culture might be the frame in which he and his supporters could organize. But very soon the idea of the International Fraternity for Ethics and Culture was to be replaced by the International Fraternity for Psychoanalysis, called "The International Psychoanalytic Association."

[1] Jones, *op. cit.,* Vol. II, p. 67.
[2] *Ibid.*

This Association was founded in a spirit quite different from what is usual for a scientific society. It was to be organized along rather dictatorial lines. Before the congress, Ferenczi had written Freud that "the psychoanalytical outlook does not lead to a democratic equalizing: there should be an elite rather on the lines of Plato's rule of the philosophers [Letter to Freud, February 5, 1910]." Freud answered three days later that he had already had the same idea.[3] Ferenczi went a step further in implementing this general principle. After proposing the formation of an international association, with branch societies in various countries, Ferenczi asserted the necessity "for all papers written or addresses delivered by any psychoanalyst to be first submitted for approval." [4] Even though this proposal was too extreme to be accepted, it is symptomatic of the spirit of the movement which Freud started with Ferenczi, from the very beginning.

The second psychoanalytic congress had all the earmarks of a political convention. "The discussion that arose after Ferenczi's paper was," according to Jones, "so acrimonious that it had to be postponed to the next day." [5] Things got worse, when the proposition was made to give the positions of president and secretary to Swiss analysts, the long and faithful services of the Viennese being ignored.

Freud himself perceived the advantage of establishing a broader basis for the work than could be

[3] Both letters quoted from Jones, *op. cit.*, Vol. II, p. 68.
[4] *Ibid.*, p. 69.
[5] *Ibid.*

provided by Viennese Jewry, and that it was necessary to convince his Viennese colleagues of this.
Hearing that several of them were holding a protest
meeting in Stekel's hotel room, he went up to join
them and made an impassioned appeal for their adherence. He laid stress on the virulent hostility that
surrounded them and the need for outside support
to counter it. Then, dramatically throwing back his
coat, he declared: "My enemies would be willing to
see me starve; they would tear my coat off my
back." [6]

Aside from Freud's starvation complex in connection
with which I first quoted this paragraph, we see here the
dramatic and somewhat hysterical gesture of the political leader to force his adherents into acceptance of the
idea that psychoanalysis was to be a world-wide movement and therefore had to change its leadership from the
hands of the Viennese Jews into those of the Swiss Gen-
tiles. Jung had to become, as it were, the Paul of the new
religion. But Freud took also political steps

for appeasing the two leaders of the revolt. He announced his retirement from the Presidency of the
Viennese Society in which he would be replaced by
Adler. He also agreed that, partly so as to counter-
balance Jung's editorship of the *Jahrbuch*, a new
periodical be founded, the monthly *Zentralblatt für
Psychoanalyse* which would be edited jointly by Adler and Stekel. They then calmed down, agreed to

[6] *Ibid.,* pp. 69–70.

his being Director of the new periodical and to Jung being made president of the Association.[7]

From this description it can be easily inferred that what motivated Freud, Ferenczi and the others was the enthusiasm of men leading a quasi-religious movement, holding conventions, conclaves, attacking and appeasing, rather than the attitude of scientists concerned with the discussion of their subject matter. A similar political spirit can be recognized a little later in Freud's dealing with the great psychiatrist, Bleuler. At the end of this same year, Freud wrote to Pfister: "I have taken great trouble wtih Bleuler. I can not say that I want to hold him to us *at any cost,* since after all Jung is rather close to me, but I will willingly sacrifice for Bleuler anything provided it could not harm our cause. Unfortunately I have little hope." [8]

After the first years of unity, dissension began to split the ranks of the movement. On the surface these dissentions arose over matters of theoretical opinion. But had this been the only aspect, there would hardly have been the bitterness which accompanied these events. Certainly to a large extent dissensions and the mood around them were conditioned by the ambitions of the dissenters to be heads of new sects, but equally so by the political and fanatical spirit of Freud and his followers. However, the form these dissensions and schisms took was the outcome not only of Freud's and his opponents' characters, but of the structure the movement had assumed. In a

[7] *Ibid.*
[8] Quoted, *ibid.,* p. 73.

hierarchically organized movement, out to conquer the world for its ideal, these methods are logical. They are the same as in other aggressive religious and political movements centered around a dogma and the idolization of the leader.

The break with Jung, more dangerous politically and more harmful to Freud personally than any of the other dissensions, led to a new tightening of the movement by the foundation of a secret international committee of seven (including Freud) that was to watch and influence the course of the movement. The unusual idea of such a committee shows the political spirit the movement had assumed. The plan came from Ferenczi. Already in 1912, after the defection of Adler and Stekel, and after Freud had said in July of that year that his relations to Jung were beginning to be strained, Ferenczi remarked to Jones "that the ideal plan would be for a number of men who had been thoroughly analyzed by Freud personally to be stationed in different centers or countries. There seemed to be no prospect of this, however, so I [Jones] proposed that in the meantime we form a small group of trustworthy analysts as a sort of Old Guard around Freud. It would give him the assurance that only a stable body of firm friends could, it would be a comfort in the event of further dissensions." [9] The proposal was heartily concurred in by Rank and Abraham. Again it is characteristic of the movement that at the very same time this proposal was discussed, Ferenczi asked Rank whether he would remain loyal to the movement and wrote Freud the following about Jones: "You must keep

[9] *Ibid.*, p. 152.

Jones constantly under your eye and cut off his line of retreat." [10]

Freud himself was enthusiastic about the idea and answered Jones's letter immediately.

> What took hold of my imagination immediately is your idea of a secret council composed of the best and most truthworthy among our men to take care of the further development of psychoanalysis and defend the cause against personalities and accidents when I am no more. . . . I dare say it would make living and dying easier for me if I knew of such an association existing to watch over my creation. First of all: This committee would have to be *strictly secret* in its existence and in its actions. . . . Whatever the next time may bring, the future foreman of the psychoanalytical movement might come out of this small but select circle of men, in whom I am still ready to confide in spite of my last disappointments with men.[11]

A year later the committee assembled for the first time as a whole, consisting of Jones, Ferenczi, Abraham, Rank and Sachs. Freud celebrated the event by presenting each one with an antique Greek intaglio from his collection, which they then got mounted in a gold ring. Freud himself had long worn such a ring and, when Eitingon some years later was also given one, there were the Seven Rings of which Sachs speaks in his book.

[10] Letter to Freud from Ferenczi, August 6, 1912, quoted by Jones, *ibid.*, p. 153.
[11] Letter to Jones, August 1, 1912, quoted by Jones, *ibid.*, p. 154.

The further development of the movement followed the path indicated by the events until, and including, the formation of the committee. In his "On the History of the Psychoanalytic Movement," Freud betrays clearly the quasi-political spirit of the movement. He enumerates the various conquests of the movement in several countries. Expressing satisfaction on the progress in America, he adds, characteristically: "But it is clear that precisely for this reason the centres of ancient culture, where the greatest resistance has been displayed, must be the scene *for the final, decisive battle for psychoanalysis.*" [12] Or he writes about his fight with his opponents: "The story [of the opposition to psychoanalysis] is not very creditable to the scientific men of our time. But to this I will immediately add that it has never occurred to me to pour contempt upon the opponents of psychoanalysis merely because they were opponents, apart from the few paltry creatures, swindlers and adventurers who are always found on both sides in times of war." [13] Freud then describes the necessity for a "leader," assuming that many of the pitfalls lying in wait for anyone who undertakes psychoanalysis "might be avoided if someone prepared to instruct and admonish could be established in a position of authority. . . . There should be some headquarters whose duty it would be to announce: 'All this nonsense had nothing to do with psychoanalysis.' " [14]

An international organization was built with branches in many countries and strict rules as to who had a right

[12] S. Freud, "On the History of the Psychoanalytic Movement," in *Collected Papers,* Vol. I, p. 316.
[13] *Ibid.,* p. 324.
[14] *Ibid.,* pp. 329–30.

to consider himself a psychoanalyst. We see here the spectacle, so rare in other scientific fields, of the progress of a scientific theory being chained to the discoveries of its founder for decades, and no freedom given to revise certain fundamental theses of the master.

Even the language used by Freud has this quasi-political character. Thus he speaks of a congress in 1910 as of the "Nuremberg *Reichstag*," which "closes the childhood of our movement." [15] And when Jung became, in Freud's opinion, too interested in the interpretation of myths, Freud warned him, and wrote to Jones about this warning (January 22, 1911):

> I am more than ever convinced that he is the man of the future. His own investigations have carried him far into the realm of mythology, which he wants to open up with the key of the libido theory. However agreeable all that may be, I nevertheless bade him in good time to return to the neuroses. There is the *motherland* where we have first to *fortify our dominion against all things and everybody*. [16]

These other fields Freud often spoke of as the *colonies* of psychoanalysis, not the *motherland*. [17] This is, indeed, the language of an empire builder or political leader. The boy who admired Marshal Masséna, the adolescent who wanted to be a liberal or socialist political leader, the grown-up man, who identified himself with Hannibal

[15] Letter to Ferenczi (April 3, 1910), quoted by Jones, *op cit.*, Vol. II, p. 71.
[16] *Ibid.*, p. 140. (My italics. E. F.)
[17] *Ibid.*

and Moses, saw in his creation, the psychoanalytic movement, the instrument to save—and to conquer—the
world for an ideal.

The answer to the question what this ideal was is not
easy to give. Freud and his adherents repressed the awareness of their mission. Their idea did not lend itself directly to such quasi-religious purposes. It was a method
of therapy and the psychological theory of the unconscious, of repression, resistance, transference, dream interpretation, etc. There was nothing explicit which could
form the nucleus of a faith. The content of this faith
remained always *implicit*. Explicitly, Freud denied that
psychoanalysis was any *Weltanschauung,* any philosophy
of life. "Psychoanalysis," he said, "is not in my opinion
in a condition to create a *Weltanschauung* of its own. It
has no need to do so, for it is a branch of science and
can subscribe to the scientific *Weltanschauung*. The latter, however, hardly merits such a high-sounding name,
for it does not take everything into its scope, it is incomplete and it makes no claim to be comprehensive or
to be constituting a system." [18] Thus Freud, according to
his own words, disclaims the existence of a particular
philosophy to which psychoanalysis gives expression; yet
considering all the facts, I can only come to the conclusion that this is what Freud *consciously* believed, and
what he wanted to believe, while his wish to have founded a new philosophical-scientific religion was repressed
and thus unconscious.

Yet, the same Freud wrote in a moving letter to Ferenczi (March 8, 1913): "It is quite possible that this

[18] S. Freud, *New Introductory Lectures on Psychoanalysis,* W. W.
Norton & Co., New York, 1933, p. 248.

time we shall be really buried, after a burial hymn has so often been sung over us in vain. That will change a great deal in our personal fate, but nothing in that of Science. *We possess the truth;* I am as sure of it as fifteen years ago." [19]

What was this truth? What was the nucleus of this psychoanalytic religion, what was the dogma from which sprang the energies to found and spread the movement?

I believe this central dogma is most clearly expressed by Freud in *The Ego and the Id:* "The development of the Ego progresses from the recognition of the instincts to their domination, from obedience to them to their inhibition. The Super-Ego, being partly reaction formation against the instinctual processes in the Id, participates greatly in this achievement. *Psychoanalysis is the instrument destined for the progressive conquest of the Id."* [20] Freud expresses here a religious-ethical aim, the conquest of passion by reason. This aim has roots in Protestantism, in Enlightenment philosophy, in the philosophy of Spinoza and in the religion of Reason, but it assumed its specific form in Freud's concept. Up to Freud the attempt had been made to dominate man's irrational affects by reason, without knowing them, or rather without knowing their deeper sources. Freud, believing that he had discovered these sources in the libidinous strivings and their complicated mechanisms of repression, sublimation, symptom formation, etc., had to believe that now, for the first time, the age-old dream of man's self-control and rationality could be realized. To form an analogy with Marx: just as Marx believed he had found

[19] Jones, *op. cit.*, Vol. II, p. 148.
[20] *The Ego and the Id,* Ch. 5. (My italics. E. F.)

the *scientific* basis for socialism, in contrast to what he called *utopian socialism,* Freud felt that he had found the scientific basis for an old moral aim and thus progressed over the *utopian morality* presented by religions and philosophies. Since he had no faith in the average man, this new scientific morality was an aim to be accomplished only by the elite, and the psychoanalytic movement was the active *avant-garde,* small but well-organized, to bring about the victory of the moral ideal.

Perhaps Freud could have become a socialist leader or the leader of an ethical culture movement, or, for other reasons, a leader of the Zionist movement; he could have —yet he could not have, since aside from his wish to solve the riddle of human existence, he had an all-absorbing scientific interest in the human mind, had started a career as a physician and was too sensitive and skeptical to be a political leader. But under the disguise of a scientific school, he realized his old dream, to be the Moses who showed the human race the promised land, the conquest of the Id by the Ego, and the way to this conquest.

IX.

Freud's Religious and Political Convictions

IT IS interesting at this point to raise the question of what Freud's own religious and political convictions were. The answer as to his religious conviction is simple, since he has made his attitude very explicit in various writings, especially in the *Future of an Illusion.* He sees in the belief in God a fixation to the longing for an all-protecting father figure, an expression of a wish to be helped and saved, when in reality man can, if not save himself, at least help himself, only by waking up from childish illusions and by using his own strength, his reason and skills.

Freud's political attitude is more difficult to describe, because he never gave any systematic account of it. It is also more complex and contradictory than his attitude toward religion. On the one hand one can clearly discern the radical tendencies in Freud. As mentioned before, in his schooltime friendship with Heinrich Braun, he was probably impressed by socialist ideas. When, before his entry to the university, he planned to study law in order to have the chance for a political career, he was certainly prompted by his enthusiasm for the ideas of political liberalism. The same sympathy must have been present in his interest in J. S. Mill, whom he translated, and must have still existed in 1910 when he played with the idea of joining, together with other analysts, the International Fraternity for Ethics and Culture.

But in spite of his earlier liberal or even socialist sympathies, Freud's picture of man never transcended that of the nineteenth-century middle class. In fact, his whole psychological system cannot be fully appreciated unless we examine the social philosophy upon which it was built.

Let us consider first Freud's concept of sublimation.

By non-satisfaction of instinctual desires, so Freud thought, by self-deprivation, the elite, in contrast to the mob, "saves" the psychic capital for cultural achievements. The whole mystery of sublimation, which Freud never quite adequately explained, is the mystery of capital formation according to the myth of the nineteenth-century middle class. Just as wealth is the product of saving, culture is the product of instinctual frustration.

Another part of the nineteenth-century picture of man was also fully accepted by Freud and translated into his psychological theory; I mean the picture of man as being basically aggressive and competitive. Freud expressed these ideas very clearly in his analysis of culture, *Civilization and Its Discontents*.

Homo homini lupus; who has the courage to dispute it in the face of all the evidence in his own life and in history? This aggressive cruelty usually lies in wait for some provocation, or else it steps into the service of some other purpose, the aim of which might as well have been achieved by earlier measures. In circumstances that favor it, when those forces in the mind which ordinarily inhibit it cease to operate, it also manifests itself spontaneously and reveals men as savage beasts to whom the thought of sparing their own kind is alien.[1]

This natural aggressiveness in man leads to another trait, central to the then current picture of man, his inherent competiveness. "Civilized society is perpetually menaced with disintegration through this primary hostility of men towards one another." [2] This hostility is only apparently founded in economic inequality. "By abolishing private property one deprives the human love of aggression of one of its instruments, a strong one, undoubtedly, but assuredly not the strongest." What, then, is the strongest source of human—or rather, male—competitiveness? It is the males' wish for unrestricted and unlimited access to all females they might desire. Originally, it is the competition between father and sons for Mother; then it is the competition among the sons for all accessible women. "Suppose that personal rights to material goods are done away with, there still remain prerogatives in sexual relationships, which must arouse the strongest rancour and most violent enmity among men and women who are otherwise equal." [3]

For the middle-class thinkers of Freud's time, man

[1] *Civilization and Its Discontents,* pp. 86–87.
[2] *Ibid.,* pp. 85–86.
[3] *Ibid.,* pp. 88–89.

was primarily isolated and self-sufficient. Inasmuch as he needed certain commodities he had to go to the market, to meet with other individuals who needed what he had to sell and who had to sell what he needed—and this mutually profitable exchange constitutes the essence of social coherence. In his libido theory, Freud expressed the same idea in psychological, rather than in economic terms. Man is basically a machine, driven by libido and regulating itself by the need to reduce painful tension to a certain minimal threshold. This reduction of tension constitutes the nature of pleasure. In order to arrive at this satisfaction, men and women need each other. They become engaged in mutual satisfaction of their libidinous needs, and this constitutes their interest in each other. However, they remain basically isolated beings, just as vendor and buyer on the market do; while they are drawn to each other by the need to satisfy their instinctual desires, they never transcend their fundamental separateness. Man, for Freud, as for most other thinkers of his time, was a social animal only by the necessity for the mutual satisfaction of his needs, not by any primary need to be related to one another.

This description of the connection between Freud's and the nineteenth-century middle class's picture of man would not be complete without mentioning an essential concept of Freud's theory, that of the "economic aspect" of the libido. Libido, for Freud, is always a fixed quantity, which can be spent in this or that way, but which is subject to the laws of matter: what is spent cannot be recovered. This lies behind concepts like narcissism, where it is a matter of *either* sending out libido to the outside, *or* taking it back to my own ego; it lies behind the concept of destructive impulses being directed *either* toward others, *or* myself; and it lies behind Freud's concept of the impossibility of brotherly love. In a passage, quoted before, he explains in terms of this concept of fixed quantities the absurdity of the commandment: "Love thy neighbor as thyself."

> My love seems to me a valuable thing that I have no right to throw away without reflection. . . . I shall even be doing wrong if I do, for my love is valued as a privilege by all those belonging to me; it is an injustice to them, if I put a stranger on the same level with them. But if I am to love him (with that kind of universal love) simply because he, too, is a denizen of the earth, like an insect or an earthworm, or a grass-snake, then I fear that but a *small modicum of love will fall to his lot,* and it would be impossible for me to give him as much as by all the laws of reason I am entitled to retain for myself.[4]

It hardly needs further comment to show that Freud speaks here of love as a man of his time speaks of property or capital. In fact, he uses the exact argument, often used against a misunderstood socialism: if all capitalists divided their money among the poor, everybody would receive only a small sum.

The nineteenth-century economist as well as the average man had a picture of the nature of man which tended to prove that contemporary capitalism is the best answer to man's existence, because it satisfies the drives inherent in human nature. The ideologists of any given

[4] *Ibid.,* pp. 81–82.

society do this, and have to do it, because the acceptance of a given social order is greatly furthered by the belief that the order is a natural, hence a necessary and good one. What I wanted to point out is that Freud did not transcend the notion of man current in his society. He even gave new weight to the current concepts by showing how they were rooted in the very nature of the libido and its operation. Freud was, in this respect, the psychologist of nineteenth-century society, who showed that the assumptions about man underlying the economic system were even more right than the economists could have imagined. His concept of Homo sexualis was a deepened and enlarged version of the economist's concept of Homo economicus. Only in one respect did Freud deviate from the traditional picture: he declared that the degree of sexual repression assumed to be normal in his time was excessive, and actually causing neurosis. In this respect, however, he was not questioning the basic picture of man, but, like all liberal reformers, trying to mitigate man's burden within the very framework of the traditional picture of man.

While Freud's *theoretical* picture of man's nature was the same as that of the majority of his contemporaries, there was also no difference in his *political* attitude, especially not toward the First World War, that supreme test, not only for the heart, but also for the reason and realism of men at that time. "Freud's immediate response to the declaration of war," writes Jones,

was an unexpected one. One would have supposed that a pacific *savant* of fifty eight would have greeted it with simple horror, as so many did. On the contrary, his first response was rather one of youthful enthusiasm, apparently an awakening of the military ardors of his boyhood. He even referred to [Austrian Foreign Minister] Berchthold's reckless action as "a release of tension through a boldspirited deed", ("Das Befreiende der mutigen Tat.") and said that for the first time in thirty years he felt himself to be an Austrian. . . . He was quite carried away, could not think of any work, and spent his time discussing the events of the day with his brother Alexander. As he put it: "All my libido is given to Austro-Hungary." [5]

He, characteristically, compared the events of the war with the war of his movement. In a letter to Hitschmann he wrote: "We have won the campaign against the Swiss, but I wonder if the Germans will end the war victoriously and if we shall be able to hold out till then. We must strongly hope so. The rage of the Germans seems to be a guarantee for it, and the Austrian re-birth is promising." [6]

It is characteristic of Jones's idolatry, but also of the orthodox point of view, that the moral and political problem of Freud's war enthusiasm is camouflaged by the "interpretation" that we deal with here, with a "youthful enthusiasm, apparently an awakening of the military ardors of his boyhood." Jones may have felt a little embarrassed to have to report this reaction of Freud's, and so he writes that "this mood, however, lasted little more

[5] E. Jones, *op. cit.*, Vol. II, p. 171. (Letter to Abraham, July 26, 1914.)

[6] *Ibid.* (Letter to Hitschmann, August 1914.)

than a fortnight and Freud came to himself." [7] But this
happens not to be the case, as Jones's further report in-
dicates. First of all, he "came to his senses" only as far
as this enthusiasm for Austria was concerned, and for a
motive which was not too reasonable either. "Curiously
enough," writes Jones, "what brought about the reversal
of Freud's feelings was a loathing for the incompetence
his newly adopted fatherland was displaying in its campaign against the Serbians." [8] But, as far as Germany was
concerned, it took some more years, and not a fortnight,
until he gave up his enthusiasm. Still in 1918, Freud
wished for a German victory, although by that time it
seemed to him improbable.[9] Only at the very end of the
war did he overcome his illusions. But in contrast with
many others, the experience of the First World War, and
probably his own self-deception in it, must have had a
profound and clarifying effect on Freud. In the early thirties, in a remarkable exchange of letters with Albert
Einstein on the question whether anything could be done
to prevent future wars, he speaks of himself and of Einstein as of pacifists, and leaves no doubt as to his antago-
nism to war. While he sees the readiness of man to en-
gage in war as rooted in the death instinct, he states that
with growing civilization the destructive tendencies become increasingly internalized (in the form of the super-
ego) and he expresses the hope that it is perhaps not a
utopian idea that the internalization of aggression and a

[7] *Ibid.*
[8] *Ibid.*, p. 172.
[9] Letter to Abraham, March 22, 1918, quoted by E. Jones, *op.
cit.*, Vol. III, p. 195.

horror of the devastation caused by another war might put an end to all wars in a not too distant future.[10]

But at the same time, Freud manifests in his letter to Einstein a political attitude far to the right of liberalism, an attitude which he had expressed also in the *Future of an Illusion*. He declares that it is an aspect of the constitutional and unchangeable inequality of men that they are divided into leaders and dependents. The latter, the vast majority, need an authority which makes decisions for them, to which they submit more or less unconditionally. The only hope is that this elite would consist of people who form an aristocracy of men, capable of using their brains, and without fear in the battle for truth. The ideal would naturally be "a community of men who had subordinated their instinctual life to the dictatorship of reason." [11]

Again we recognize Freud's fundamental ideal of the domination of instinct by reason, mixed with deep disbelief in the power of the average man to direct his own destiny. This is one of the tragic aspects of Freud's life: that a year before Hitler's victory he despairs of the possibility of democracy, and offers the dictatorship of the elite of courageous, self-frustrating men as the only hope. Was this not the hope that only the psychoanalyzed elite could direct and control the indolent masses?

[10] Cf. *Why War?*, 1932, *Collected Papers*, Vol. V, pp. 273–288.
[11] *Ibid.*, p. 284.

X.

Summary and Conclusion

THE foregoing analysis has tried to show that Freud's aim was to found a movement for the ethical liberation of man, a new secular and scientific religion for an elite which was to guide mankind.

But Freud's own messianic impulses could not have transformed psychoanalysis into the Movement had it not been for the needs of his followers and eventually those of the wide public which became enthusiastically attracted to psychoanalysis.

Who were these first most loyal disciples, the wearers of the six rings? They were urban intellectuals, with a deep yearning to be committed to an ideal, to a leader, to a movement, and yet without having any religious or political or philosophical ideal or convictions; there was neither a socialist, Zionist, Catholic nor Orthodox Jew among them. (Eitingon may have had mild Zionist sympathies.) Their religion was the Movement. The growing circle of analysts came from the same background; the vast majority were and are middle-class intellectuals, with no religious, political or philosophical interests or commitments. The great popularity of psychoanalysis in the West, and particularly in the United States, since the beginning of the thirties has undoubtedly the same social basis. Here is a middle class for whom life has lost meaning. They have no political or religious ideals, yet they are in search of a meaning, of an idea to devote themselves to, of an explanation of life which does not require faith or sacrifices, and which satisfies this need to feel part of a movement. All these needs were fulfilled by the Movement.[1]

But the new religion shared the fate of most religious movements. The original enthusiasm, freshness and spontaneity soon weaken; a hierarchy takes over, which gets its prestige from the "correct" interpretation of the dogma, and the power to judge who is and who is not a faithful adherent of the religion. Eventually, dogma, ritual and idolization of the leader replace creativity and spontaneity.

The tremendous role of the *dogma* in orthodox psychoanalysis hardly needs any proof. In fifty years, there has been relatively little theoretical development beyond Freud's own theoretical innovation.[2] Mainly, one has applied Freud's theories to clinical material, always with the

---

[1] H. W. Puner has made this point very succinctly in her biography. *Op. cit.,* p. 104.

[2] The one great creative revision in psychoanalytic thought, the concept of the life and death instinct, was made by Freud himself and was never fully accepted by all orthodox psychoanalysts nor further developed. Freud himself never undertook the drastic revision of his older mechanistic concepts which the new theory, in my opinion, would have made necessary. For these reasons and in view of the limited space of this study I have throughout referred only to what is the bulk of Freud's theory, the stage before the discussion of the death instinct.

tendency to prove that Freud was right, and with little thought for other theoretical possibilities. Even the most independent development, the new emphasis on the Ego, seems to be to a large extent a rephrasing of many well-known insights in terms of the Freudian theory, without leading to many new vistas. But aside from the relative sterility of the "official" psychoanalytic thought, its dogmatism is manifested in its reaction to any deviation. One of the most drastic examples, I have already given—Freud's reaction to Ferenczi's idea that the patient needed love as a condition for his cure. This only emphasized what was and is going on everywhere in the movement. Analysts who criticize Freud's ideas explicitly, frankly and publicly are considered as outside the fold, even when they have no intention of founding "schools" of their own, but only set forth the result of their thinking and observation based on those of Freud.

The *ritualistic* element in orthodox psychoanalysis is equally obvious. The couch with the chair behind it, the four or five sessions every week, the analyst's silence, except when he gives an "interpretation"—all these factors have been transformed from what once were useful means to an end, into a sacred ritual, without which orthodox psychoanalysis is unthinkable. The most striking example of this is, perhaps, the couch. Freud chose it because he "did not want to be stared at for eight hours a day." Then, other reasons were added: that the patient should not recognize the analyst's reaction to what he is telling —and, thus, that it is better if the analyst sits behind him; or, that the patient feels freer and more relaxed if he does not have to look at the analyst; or, and this has been emphasized lately, that the "couch-situation" creates artificially an infantile situation which should exist for the better development of the transference. Whatever the merits of these arguments are—I personally believe that they are not valid—in any "normal" discussion on therapeutic technique, they could be freely argued. In psychoanalytic orthodoxy failure to use the couch is already evidence of digression and considered *prima facie* evidence for not being an analyst."

Many of the patients are attracted by this very ritualism; they feel themselves to be part of the movement, experience a sense of solidarity with all others who are analyzed, and a sense of superiority over those who are not. Often, they are much less concerned with being cured than with the exhilarating sensation of having found a spiritual home.

Eventually, the *idolization of Freud's personality* completes the picture of the quasi-political character of the Movement. I can be short here and refer to Jones's idolatric picture of Freud, his denial of Freud's intense concern for public recognition, his authoritarianism and any kind of human foible. Another well-known symptom of the same complex is the habit of orthodox Freudian writers to begin, end and intersperse their scientific papers with "as Freud has already said" remarks, even when such frequent citations are quite unnecessary in the context of the paper.

I have tried to show that psychoanalysis was conceived as, and developed further into, a quasi-religious movement based on psychological theory and implemented by a psycho-therapy. This in itself is perfectly legitimate. The criticism, expressed in these pages, is directed against the inherent errors and limitations in the way psychoanalysis developed. First of all, it suffered from the very defect it aims at curing: repression. Neither Freud nor his followers admitted to others or to themselves that they aimed at more than scientific and therapeutic achievements. They repressed their ambition to conquer the world with a messianic ideal of salvation and thus were caught in ambiguities and dishonesties, which are bound to follow from such repression. The second defect of the movement was its authoritarian and fanatical character, which prevented the fruitful development of the theory of man, and led to the establishment of an entrenched bureaucracy which inherited Freud's mantle, without possessing his creativity, nor the radicalism of his original conception.

But more important still than the points mentioned so far is the *content* of the idea. Indeed, Freud's great discovery, that of a new dimension of human reality, the unconscious, is *one element* in a movement aiming at human reform. But this very discovery bogged down in a fatal way. It was applied to a small sector of reality, man's libidinal strivings and their repression, but little or not at all to the wider reality of human existence and to social and political phenomena. Most psychoanalysts, and this holds true even for Freud, are not less blind to the realities of human existence and to unconscious social phenomena than are the other members of their own social class. In a sense, they are more blind because they believe they have found *the* answer to life in the formula of libidinal repression. But one cannot see in certain sectors of human reality and remain blind in others. This is especially true since the whole phenomenon of repression is a social phenomenon. The individual in any given society represses the awareness of those feelings and phantasies which are incompatible with the thought patterns of his society. The force effecting this repression is the fear of being isolated and of becoming an outcast through having thoughts and feelings which nobody would share. (In the extreme form the fear of complete isolation is no other than the fear of insanity.) Considering this, it is imperative for the psychoanalyst to transcend the thought patterns of his society, to look at them critically, and to understand the realities which produce these patterns. *The understanding of the unconscious of the individual presupposes and necessitates the critical analysis of his society.* The very fact that Freudian psychoanalysis hardly ever transcended a liberal middle-class attitude toward society constitutes one reason for its narrowness and for the eventual stagnation in its proper field of the understanding of the individual unconscious. (There is, incidentally, a strange—though negative—connection between orthodox Freudian and orthodox Marxist theory: Freudians saw the individual unconscious, and were blind to the social unconscious; orthodox Marxists, on the contrary, were keenly aware of the unconscious factors in social behavior, but remarkably blind in their appreciation of individual motivation. This led to a deterioration of Marxist theory and practice, just as the reverse phenomenon has led to the deterioration of psychoanalytic theory and therapy. This result should not surprise anybody. Whether one studies society or individuals, one always deals with human beings, and that means that one deals with their unconscious motivations; one cannot separate man as an individual from man as a social participant—and if one does, one ends up by understanding neither.)

What, then, is our conclusion with regard to the role which Freudian psychoanalysis has played since the beginning of the century?

First of all, it must be noted that in the beginning, from 1900 to the twenties, psychoanalysis was much more radical than it became after it had gained its great popularity. For the middle class brought up in the Victorian age, Freud's statements about infantile sexuality, the pathological effects of sexual repression, etc., were radical violations of their taboos, and it took courage and independence to violate these taboos. But thirty years later, when the twenties had brought with them a wave of sexual libertinism and a widespread abandonment of Victorian standards, the very same theories were no longer shocking or challenging. Thus, psychoanalytic theory gained popular acclaim in all those sectors of society which were averse to genuine radicalism, that is, to going "to the roots," and yet which were eager to criticize and to transgress the conservative mores of the nineteenth century. In these circles—that is to say, among the liberals—psychoanalysis expressed the desirable middle-of-the-road attitude between humanist radicalism and Victorian conservatism. Psychoanalysis became a substitute satisfaction for a deep human yearning, that of finding a meaning to life, of being in genuine touch with reality, of doing away with the distortions and projections which put a veil between reality and ourselves. Psychoanalysis became a surrogate for religion for the urban middle and upper-middle classes, which did not want to make a more radical and comprehensive

effort. Here, in the Movement, they found everything—
a dogma, a ritual, a leader, a hierarchy, the feeling of
possessing the truth, of being superior to the uninitiated;
yet without great effort, without deeper comprehension
of the problems of human existence, without insight into
and criticism of their own society and its crippling effects
on man, without having to change one's character in
those aspects which matter, namely to get rid of one's
greed, anger and folly. All one tried to get rid of were
certain libidinous fixations and their transference, and
while this may sometimes be significant, it is not sufficient
for the achievement of that characterological change
which is necessary to be in full touch with reality. From
a forward-moving and courageous idea, psychoanalysis
became transformed into the safe credo of those frightened and isolated members of the middle class who did
not find a haven in the more conventional religious and
social movements of the time. The decay of liberalism is
expressed in the decay of psychoanalysis.

It has often been said that the changes in sexual mores
which took place after the First World War were in themselves a result of the increasing popularity of psychoanalytic doctrines. I think this assumption is quite er-
roneous. Needless to say Freud was never a spokesman
for sexual libertinism. On the contrary, he was, as I tried
to show before, a man whose ideal it was to control passion by reason and who, in his own attitude toward sex,
lived up to the ideal of Victorian sexual mores. He was
a liberal reformer inasmuch as he criticized Victorian
sexual morality for being too harsh and thus sometimes
producing neurosis, but this is something quite different
from the sexual freedom which the twenties ushered in.

These new sexual mores have many roots, but the most important one lies in an attitude which modern capitalism developed in the last decades, the craving for ever-increasing consumption. While the middle class of the nineteenth century was dominated by the principle to save, the middle class of the twentieth century obeys the rule of consumption, the principle of consuming immediately, without postponing the satisfaction of any wish longer than absolutely necessary.[3] This attitude refers to the consumption of commodities, just as much as to the satisfaction of sexual needs. In a society built around the maximal and immediate satisfaction of all needs, there can be little distinction between the various spheres of needs. Psychoanalytic theories—rather than being the cause of this development—offered a convenient rationalization for this trend, as far as sexual needs are concerned. If repression and frustration of needs could be a cause of neurosis, then frustration has to be avoided by all means—which is exactly what the advertising people preach anyway. Thus psychoanalysis owes its popularity as a messenger of sexual freedom to the new consumer passion, rather than being the cause of the new sexual morality.

Considering that the aim of the Movement was to help man to control his irrational passions by reason, this misuse of psychoanalysis points to a tragic defeat of Freud's hope. Even though the libertinistic mood of the twenties gave way to more conservative mores afterward, the development of sexual morality as Freud could observe it

[3] This point has been brilliantly expressed by Aldous Huxley in his *Brave New World;* cf. also the discussion of the same point in my *The Sane Society.*

during his lifetime was certainly not what he had envisaged as a desirable effect of his movement. But still more tragic is the fact that reason, the goddess of the nineteenth century, to whose realization in man the efforts of psychoanalysis were devoted, had lost the great battle between 1914 and 1939. The First World War, the victory of Nazism and Stalinism and the beginning of the Second World War are so many stations of the defeat of reason and sanity. Freud, the proud leader of the movement which aimed at the establishment of a world of reason, had to witness an era of ever-increasing social insanity.

He was the last great representative of rationalism, and his tragic fate was to end his life when this rationalism had been defeated by the most irrational forces the Western world had witnessed since the time of the witch trials. Yet, although only history can pronounce the final judgment, I believe that the tragedy in Freud's role is more the personal one of closing his life during the madness of Hitlerism and Stalinism, and in the shadows of the holocaust of the Second World War, rather than the failure of his mission. Even though his movement deteriorated into a new religion for those who sought for a refuge in a world filled with anxiety and confusion, Western thought is impregnated with Freud's discoveries, and its future is unthinkable without the fruits of this impregnation. I am speaking not only about the obvious fact that he has given a new basis for psychological theory in his discovery of the unconscious, and its mode of operation in dreams, symptoms, character traits, myths and religion, the significance of early childhood experiences for the development of character, and many other, perhaps less fundamental discoveries, but about his influence on Western thought in general.

While Freud represented the culmination of rationalism, he struck at the same time a fatal blow against rationalism. By showing that the sources of man's actions lie in the unconscious, in a depth most of which is never open to the inspecting eye, and that man's conscious thought controls his behavior only to a small degree, he undermined the rationalistic picture that man's intellect dominated the scene without restriction or challenge. In this respect, the vision of the power of the forces of the "underworld," Freud was an heir of romanticism, the movement which tried to penetrate the sphere of the non-rational. Freud's historical position, then, may be described as creating the synthesis between the two contradictory forces which dominated eighteenth- and nineteenth-century Western thought, those of Rationalism and Romanticism.

But in order to appreciate fully Freud's historical function, we must still take one further step. Freud's total approach to man was part—and perhaps the culmination —of the most important trend in Western thought since the seventeenth century: the attempt to grasp and be in touch with reality, and to rid man of the illusions which veil and distort reality. Spinoza had laid the foundations for this endeavor in his new concept of psychology which dealt with man's mind as part of nature and operating according to the laws of nature. The natural sciences, crowned by the new insights into the nature of matter, constitute another attack with the same aim. Kant, Nietzsche, Marx, Darwin, Kierkegaard, Bergson, Joyce, Picasso are other names marking the same approach to the undistorted and immediate grasp of reality. Different as they are among themselves, they are the expression of the passionate outburst of Western man's desire to relinquish false gods, to do away with illusions and to grasp himself and the world as part of a total reality. This is the aim of science on the intellectual plane as it is—on the experiential plane—the aim of the purest and most rational forms of monotheistic and particularly of Eastern non-theistic mysticism.

Freud's discoveries are an integral part of this liberating movement. Even though they were transformed into new rationalizations by a frightened generation who had lost the passionate desire for the grasp of reality which had filled Freud, the future development of mankind, if it is to survive the dark period of irrationality and insanity we are passing through, is bound up with the new insights Freud has contributed.

In leaving this book which has dealt with Freud's personality and his mission, we might look back at his towering figure, forget about the legends, idolization and hostility which have obscured his picture, and see him as the human being he was.

We see him as a person with a passionate thirst for truth, unbounded faith in reason, and unflinching courage to stake everything on this faith. We find him a man deeply in need of motherly love, admiration and protection, full of self-confidence when these are bestowed on him, depressed and hopeless when they are missing. This insecurity, both emotionally and materially, makes him seek to control others who depend on him, so that he can depend on them.

This insecurity may also be the factor in directing his

energies to obtaining the regard of the outer world. He believes that he does not care; he thinks that he is above this striving for recognition; yet this need to find recognition and fame, the bitterness when his expectations are not met, are powerful strivings in his personality.

His method of attack in the world is vigorous. His defense is a flanking movement of speed and penetration. He looks at life as an intellectual guessing game which he is determined to win by his superior intellect. In the ideas with which he works he searches for deeper values and meanings. His inner struggle with ambition and his sense of values, which often are in conflict, create an agonizing soul activity. And there is also the melancholic sense that the price of achievement is beyond its worth.

He has ability to act with an enthusiastic expenditure of all his available energy and also an insatiable capacity for experimentation in all fields and relationships. He often asserts himself in petty details and quarrels with those who do not welcome his ideas and help. He also has an instinctive feeling that he is too impressionable, and, in an effort to seem more independent than he is, will quarrel unnecessarily with those who impress him most forcibly.

Energies and ambitions are always in battle. Enmity and anger disturb him more than the average person, even though his self-control is also stronger than that of the average man. He can be diplomatic and yielding, yet at the same time he is one of the most undiplomatic persons imaginable, often stubborn, or doing something just to see the fireworks.

He has an ability to concentrate readily and to master many things. This, in its best manifestations, likens him to Goethe's universal man; in its worst, makes him a dilettante; but even then this gives him an ability to salvage and emerge with something. He is alert to general potentials and objectives, interested and encouraged by situations of great sweep or high potentiality, but he requires a method of expression that is independent. He resents interference fiercely; this sometimes leads to considerable eccentricity and conceit, and yet, at the same time, he has a delicacy of touch which is expressed in his style and in his ability to read his opponent's mind and to anticipate his actions. He wavers between the capacity for an unlimited scope of human knowing and a hopelessly opinionated and phantastic approach to people and ideas. He has the ability to arouse enthusiasm and blind devotion in others, to strike a dramatic figure, sometimes acting like a genius, sometimes like a fanatic. He has a remarkable faculty for bringing things to completion by a ruthless elimination of all side interests or of all time-consuming personal affections.

He is not a man who loves; he is egocentric, filled with the idea of his mission, expecting others to follow him, wait on him, to sacrifice their independence and intellectual freedom for him. The world is only the stage for the drama of the Movement and his mission. He is not proud of himself as a person, but of his mission, of the greatness of his cause and of himself, inasmuch as he is the bearer of the message. He experiences life, fearing the pain of losing what he has enjoyed. So he avoids joy and pleasure, and chooses as his aim the control of all passions, affects, feelings by will and reason. His ideal is the self-contained and self-controlled man, high above the rabble, renouncing the joys of life, but enjoying the security of the feeling that nobody and nothing can hurt him. He is intemperate in his relations with others and in his ambitions, and paradoxically even in his austerity he is intemperate.

He is a lonely man, and unhappy when not actively pursuing his discoveries and his quasi-political aims. He is kind and humorous, except when he feels challenged or attacked; altogether a tragic figure in one essential aspect, which he sees sharply himself; he wants to show man a promised land of reason and harmony, and yet he can only visualize it from afar; he knows he will never get there, and he probably senses, after the defection of Joshua-Jung, that those who stay with him will not get to the promised land either. One of the great men and pathfinders of the human race, he has to die with a deep sense of disappointment, yet his pride and dignity were never dented by illness, defeat and disappointment. For more independent minds than were his loyal followers, Freud was probably a difficult person to live with or even to like; yet his gifts, his honesty, his courage and the tragic character of his life may fill one not only with respect and admiration, but with loving compassion for a truly great man.

Other Black Cat Books

FEMALE HOMOSEXUALITY:

    A modern study of Lesbianism by Frank S. Caprio BC-27 75¢
The most complete and authoritative work on its subject, this book is based on hundreds of interviews with lesbians, information gathered in travels around the world, and years of clinical research. It answers the need for a comprehensive study in non-technical language.

A MAN AGAINST INSANITY by Paul de Kruif   BB-28 60¢
The story of a doctor who conquered his own insanity and now shows others the way back, by the author of *Microbe Hunters.* "An old master Paul de Kruif surely is. His latest book has pace, it has style, it has a sharply drawn hero, and, most important, it tells one of the great stories of our times."—*Washington Post and Times Herald*

BRIGHTER THAN A THOUSAND SUNS by Robert Jungk BC-29 75¢
The story of the men who made The Bomb, this is one of the most dramatic books ever published. "One of the most interesting books I have ever read. It is more exciting than any novel and, at the same time, it is packed with information which is both new and valuable."—Bertrand Russell

A LAYMAN'S GUIDE TO PSYCHIATRY AND PSYCHOANALYSIS
                        by Eric Berne BC-30 75¢
What everybody should know about his mind and emotions: In simple and witty language, Dr. Berne explains the new science of human behavior. "This book is unique . . ."—Dr. A. A. Brill

THE NATURAL HISTORY OF LOVE by Morton M. Hunt BC-31 75¢
A brilliant panorama of the ways men and women have felt about love, from the early Greeks to the present day. ". . . a superbly written book . . . illuminating and clarifying for every reader."—*N.Y. Times Book Review*

REBEL WITHOUT A CAUSE by Robert M. Lindner   BC-32 75¢
The story of the analysis of a criminal psychopath, this brilliant book by a famed writer gave a name to a whole generation. "The most exciting and one of the most deeply and tragically human stories I have read in a long time."—*The New Republic*

If your bookseller doesn't have these Black Cat Books, you may order them by writing to Black Cat Books, Order Dept., 64 University Pl., New York 3, N. Y. Please enclose cash or money order, and add 25¢ for postage and handling.